Fiction Writer's Help Book.

Maxine Rock

CINCINNATI, OHIO

The Fiction Writer's Help Book. Copyright 1982 by Maxine Rock. Printed and bound in the United States of America. All rights reserved. No part of this book may be reproduced in any form or by any electronic or mechanical means including information storage and retrieval systems without permission in writing from the publisher, except by a reviewer who may quote brief passages in a review. Published by Writer's Digest Books, 9933 Alliance Road, Cincinnati, Ohio 45242. First edition.

Library of Congress Cataloging in Publication Data

Rock, Maxine A., 1940-
   The fiction writer's help book.

   Includes index.
   1. Fiction—Authorship. I. Title
PN3355.R59 1982   808.3   82-13502
ISBN 0-89879-090-5

Design by Christine Aulicino.

*This book is dedicated to David
and to
Lauren and Michael*

Acknowledgments

I OWE GREAT THANKS to every writer and literary professional whose name appears in this book. They gave me time, encouragement, and the benefit of many years of accumulated wisdom, knowledge, and experience. This book is a celebration of their skill.

I am especially grateful to novelists Paul Darcy Boles and Frances Statham. They gave me professional advice and assistance that will stay with me long after this book is on the shelves, and their companionship helped see me through.

A tip of the pen goes to my editors, Barbara O'Brien and Carol Cartaino, and to the other nice folks at Writer's Digest Books. I am impressed with their professionalism (and everybody promptly returns telephone calls!).

To my agent, Libby Mark: thanks for getting up early on Sunday morning to work with me.

And to Frank McGuire and Rupert LeCraw of Oxford Books in Atlanta, my heartfelt gratitude for their help, encouragement, and endless cups of Red Zinger tea. They believed in me.

Contents

21 CHAPTER 1
ALPHABET, BOOKS, AND COURSES: THE EDUCATION OF AN AUTHOR

How to find a teacher . . . do workshops work? . . . why you should join (or found) a writers' group . . . the value of observation . . . the ways reading helps your writing.

33 CHAPTER 2
TOOLS OF THE TRADE

A few words about typewriters . . . the joys of word processors . . . starting simple and counting your costs . . . how to build a writer's "tool chest" . . . what editors demand . . . stimulating your fiction factory . . . tips on tape recorders, books, and movies.

43 CHAPTER 3
FINDING GOOD FICTION IDEAS

The good old "slice of life" . . . how to base fiction on fact . . . twisting the eternal themes . . . don't scorn themes that sound familiar . . . when do ideas come . . . using life experiences . . . being influenced by the market . . . how ideas develop . . . when ideas won't work . . . the importance of craft.

CHAPTER 4
55 RICHES FROM RESEARCH

Why research is essential . . . how to research the market . . . the importance of knowing your subject . . . to the library . . . exploiting primary and secondary sources . . . firm footing for your fiction and other ways research pays off . . . ways to write and ways to *think* about writing . . . personal benefits of research.

CHAPTER 5
69 CREATING CHARACTERS

How to use people you know . . . "give a guy a reason" . . . how to interview real people for your characters . . . why shyness hurts writers . . . whether or not to rely on non-fiction for fiction . . . using bits of real people to create characters . . . believability above all.

CHAPTER 6
83 PLOTS AND PLANS

Why planning makes writing easier . . . how good writers get organized . . . when characters misbehave . . . what organization entails . . . why some writers don't outline . . . subconscious planning . . . thinking before you write . . . why outlines impress publishers . . . how flexibility helps . . . how questions help organize.

97 CHAPTER 7
BEGIN AND END
WITH A BANG

Why opening lines are critical . . . how every writer finds his own technique . . . personal preference: beginning with action or description . . . how studying journalistic leads can help . . . a discussion of tone and mood . . . hooking an editor . . . figuring out the end . . . starting with questions and ending with answers . . . don't drag it out.

109 CHAPTER 8
KEEP YOUR FICTION
FLOWING

Don't let the middle get boring . . . keeping it simple . . . film-think . . . cutting the blab . . . unnecessary and necessary dirty words . . . stopping when enough is said . . . show, don't tell . . . fiction-flow and experience . . . using different techniques . . . experimenting with emotional language . . . involving the reader . . . finding a voice . . . "street talk."

121 CHAPTER 9
SUCCESS WITH
SHORT STORIES

Thunderbolts of human awareness . . . realism is the thing . . . spotlighting people . . . testing your talent on short fiction . . . why characters are foremost . . . making money writing shorts . . . squeezing out the idea . . . suggestion, compression, and poetry.

CHAPTER 10
135   KNOW (AND SELL TO) THINE EDITOR

Why editors are in the middle . . . how sales affect professional relationships . . . writers' gripes and grumbles . . . the advantages of small publishers . . . fun at lunch . . . how to please an editor . . . being businesslike . . . bad news about publishers . . . how to sell "partials" . . . getting acquainted with an editor . . . when editors love 'em and leave 'em . . . financial pressure on editors . . . being prepared to leave an editor.

CHAPTER 11
155   AGENTS, CONTRACTS, AND THE LAW

Pushing for the First Amendment . . . writers' groups that can help . . . keeping track of libel laws . . . practicing legal self-defense . . . backing up gossip with fact . . . remembering that letters are private . . . what you can copyright . . . protecting yourself with an agent . . . contract clauses your agent ought to get for you . . . going it alone.

CHAPTER 12
173   THE WRITING LIFE

Why writers write . . . the importance of discipline . . . on being your own boss . . . conquering writer's fear . . . cool-headedness . . . self-consciousness and being afraid of feelings . . . follow-through and other useful attributes.

185 EPILOGUE:
AFTER YOU'RE PUBLISHED

When the real work begins . . . self-promotion . . . hiring a publicist . . . making friends with book buyers . . . haunting the bookstores . . . writers' help groups.

Foreword

I'VE BEEN FREELANCING for fifteen years; my work sells steadily. Other writers constantly ask, "How do you *do* it? What are your secrets?"

Solid information from any writer who *sells* is a treasure. Fiction writers, more than any others, hunger for specific, factual information about their craft. This book is meant to give it to them.

The book grew out of my experience as a writer and as a writing instructor for twelve years at Georgia State University. Published writers would often visit my class to offer tips and share problem-solving techniques. Writing became less frightening that way; when beginners hear advice from professionals who also struggle daily with the craft, writing becomes do-able and *real*. To prepare the book and capitalize on that reality, I stepped out of my role as teacher to become a gatherer, interpreter, and presenter of facts—in this case, facts on fiction. Along the way, I also picked up much useful information for, by, and about nonfiction writers, and reinforced my own notions that the line between fact and fiction writing is often enticingly thin.

STRAIGHT TO THE SOURCE . . .

I grabbed as many writers as I could, yanked them into a seat, and wrung out specifics on outlining, characterization, plot, and other technicalities of this demanding and sometimes confusing craft. Then I hunched in closer and got them to tell me how they found someone to publish their books, whether agents helped, what problems came up after publication, how much money they make, and how to handle contracts and other legal affairs of the writing life.

. . . AND OTHER EXPERTS

My goal was to let the information come, edited but undiluted, direct from professional writers. When writers couldn't supply what I was after, I turned to other experts. Each interview presents the personal experience and viewpoint of a writer, editor, agent, or other professional who is deeply involved with some aspect of fiction writing. Writers of nonfiction will also find much in these pages to help them bring drama and excitement to their words.

In some cases my interviewees seemed to be at odds. I let apparent contradictions stand, because readers should know that writers and other professionals in the field don't always agree with one another.

"Live" interviews were supplemented by quotes and information gathered from newspapers, books, and magazines. When certain writers had a lot to say, I chopped their quotes into digestible segments and placed the information in the appropriate chapters. In all, the research for this book took three years. It comes together as a practical handbook on the business of fiction writing, and the emphasis is always on specific pointers on writing and marketing fiction.

"IT JUST HAPPENS . . ."

By and large, writers are not good at talking about what they do—articulating their art. Many writers can't explain what or how they write. Some of them shrug and say they can't even explain *why*. They know it's a time-consuming, emotionally draining, and financially hazardous profession. But they just write. Most of them say the process is mystical and that "it simply happens." Whenever I heard that, I'd roll my eyes and bite my lip in frustration. What sort of nonsense is that? How can you make a living that way? "I don't know," the author would say, "I just do."

So I went to other people—agents, publishers, critics, editors, non-fiction writers—and used their insights to plug the gaps the fiction writers could not fill.

You'll find here facts on the art of writing as well as the business of writing. I've learned that the most successful authors know how to handle that blend themselves. If they don't know how, they pick agents and other professionals who can do the job for them.

A WAR OF WORDS

During the course of my research, I began to suspect that for beginners, the words "business" and "writing" are often at war. They shouldn't be. Many independent writers apparently embark on their careers with money salted away from a previous job, or supplied by outside sources. At first they are reluctant to discuss money, and some pretend they don't care about it.

It's as if getting paid for what they do is a nasty embarrassment for many young writers; they're having too much fun to think about finances. Writers of nonfiction seem to be more practical. They approach their work with a grim determination to make money, but—like the fiction writers—they are often reluctant to ask for adequate payment. But I've noticed that as soon as they get some experience—that is, as soon as they are published and paid for their work— writers scorn the idea of writing for love. The business wheels start turning, the details of contracts peck at them almost as much as the details of the craft, and writers become eager to reap a healthy profit. At that point they become "professional," and buzz with information and curiosity about writers' unions, libel insurance, contract lawyers, and other means to protect and enhance their craft.

CRAFT OR GIFT?
I persist in calling all writing a "craft," even though many authors insist it's more like an esoteric gift. A craft, to me, is an occupation. It requires skill, planning, technical know-how, and lots of hard work. Even writers who insist they never plan or organize their fiction do admit the process involves much more than the random tapping of some beguiling muse at the door of their subconscious.

Erskine Caldwell, who began writing fifty years ago and whose novels, *Tobacco Road* and *God's Little Acre*, are still hot sellers, once claimed he taught himself to write without studying the masters, without reading, and without regard for plot or character development. He said he just let his mind wander, and rapped out a single sentence. Then he wondered what would happen next.

But this apparent nonchalance masked an intense craftsman's love for language, the roots and meanings of words, and the way writing conveys emotion. Caldwell was a great rewriter, who polished his work the second time around. So, even if he can't articulate the process by which he builds his fiction, it's obvious to me that Caldwell and other successful writers pay a great deal of attention to the details of the craft.

Perhaps some writers are born with the ability to practice that craft with ease. Others need more training. All writers say they love writing; the professionals admit it's damned hard work.

EASY AND HARD
Some writers say their work is easy. Others are red-faced be-

cause they find it so hard. Jessamyn West, writing in a 1962 symposium called *The Living Novel*, said this discrepancy might be a reason why writers are so close-mouthed about what they do. They either don't want to admit they struggle, or they think their work might be shrugged off by publishers and readers if they tell anybody how simple it is to do their job. It might be, said West, that writers are afraid to delve into the mechanics of their work because others might not understand that a lot of it comes naturally. "The product should not be judged by the process," she noted, "but the minute the writer mentions process he invites this kind of judgment."

FICTION FLIES AWAY

Writers say talking about what they do breaks up the train of thought and drains the author of creativity. That's why Paul Darcy Boles, a great master of contemporary fiction, told me he would talk about anything except the novel he was working on at the moment. "I don't discuss novels in progress," he said. "It makes them fly away."

To Boles, and to all the other writers who risked letting their work "fly away" while they gave me material for this book, I owe great thanks. They taught me a lot. I hope I can transmit it to my readers.

1 | Alphabet, Books and Courses: The Education of an Author

WRITING FICTION FEELS a lot like stepping into quicksand: murky, unstable, and definitely trying to suck you in. You'll do better if you have a steady foundation on which to base your attempts. That foundation is education.

Training to be a writer doesn't necessarily take place in school. Few writers say they *learned* their trade—or art—in a classroom. They speak rather of growing into writing, much as a boy grows into his older brother's coat. You keep trying it on, flexing your muscles a little more each time, until the garment that once overwhelmed you is fitting snugly.

If you're serious about writing, you'll guide that growth by selecting the courses, books, workshops, and training programs most likely to give you specific information on writing. These formal sessions won't give birth to writing talent, but they can help shape and encourage the abilities you bring to them.

SELECT A TEACHER

Your first challenge is to find a good writing teacher. Finding a professional writer who also lectures at a local university isn't hard; the trick is to discover one who writes and who can also *teach* writing. Don't settle for a novelist who uses class sessions to read his work to a captive audience. Sit in on one or two classes before you sign up, to feel out the instructor.

Primarily, a good writing teacher is one who can tell you what's wrong (and right) about *your* work. In college, students are often tempted to pick a teacher on the basis of his personality; now you must use more objective criteria.

Here are a few guidelines: the instructor should be a published writer who is selling his work to recognized markets. One who has not written at all is bound to offer hollow advice; one who has written but not published doesn't know professional joys or problems; one who has "retired" may no longer be sufficiently afire to kindle your imagination.

Check your teacher's background and credentials. He should know the English language thoroughly. College and graduate degrees can be good evidence of this, but they're no guarantee. If your tutor reads and has devoured the classics, he might be suitable even though self-taught.

If your teacher has special honors and belongs to a variety of writers' groups requiring active participation, that's a plus.

Read what your teacher has written. Do you like his stories and novels? Are they well written and meaningful to you? It won't help if others drool over his work but you dislike it.

Last, be sure you and your teacher can get along. Nothing is worse for you than a sarcastic, hostile, or uncaring teacher.

Your teacher can be a college professor, an editor, or a practicing writer willing to read your work for an hourly fee. Fifteen to thirty-five dollars per hour is a reasonable charge, if significant, constructive comments are made on paper and returned to you with your work within about two weeks from the time you handed in your manuscript.

23 Alphabets, Books, Courses

Don't get impatient if your teacher stresses grammar. Critic/writer Thomas H. Middleton insists that many writers overlook the basic rules of grammar, and says "Writing without rules doesn't work." He points out that a teacher who doesn't correct your spelling and punctuation is a careless teacher and may not know the rules himself. What happens then?

"When writers don't know the rules, their writing usually turns to mush. When writing turns to mush, thought, which feeds on writing, suffers from malnutrition and is incapable of clear development or expression."

Good teachers are demanding. They insist not only on proper grammar, but note every misspelled word and glare at you until you use the dictionary. And they make you rewrite again and again until weak passages are eliminated and your prose marches forward with strength and assurance. A writing teacher who merely comments on your first draft without insisting on one or more rewrites could be neglecting his duty.

Writing classes or individual instruction may not be enough to sharpen your writing skills. Enroll in English literature classes headed by instructors who carefully analyze great works of fiction. The way to get the most out of such classes is to imagine them as courses in watch repair. To fix a watch you must first take it apart, then learn how to put all the pieces together again until it ticks properly. The best way to learn good fiction writing is by taking books apart, and being skillfully guided as you reconstruct them piece by piece. Sometimes no writing at all is done in classes like these. The time is devoted instead to discussing works of fiction. Ideally, you should take at least one "do it" and one "think about it" course.

Journalism courses are also helpful. They force you to cut unnecessary words, to sharpen your skills of observation and clarity of thought. Most of my formal education has been in journalism; I majored in it at New York University and earned my master's degree in journalism at the University of Michigan. Journalism courses knocked out a lot of my destructive tendencies to overwrite, and forced me to realize the importance of clean, simple sentences.

Ernest Hemingway, who served a stint as a reporter on the Kansas City *Star*, later said his ficton style was based on what he learned as a journalist. He recalled the principles of news writing as laid down in the *Star's* style book: "Use short sentences. Use short first paragraphs. Use vigorous English, not forgetting to strive for smoothness. Be positive, not negative."

Hemingway maintained that he learned those rules and stuck to them. "Those were the best rules I ever learned for the business of writing," he claimed. "I've never forgotten them. No man with any talent, who feels and writes truly about the thing he is trying to say, can fail to write well if he abides by them."

TRY OUT WORKSHOPS

Writers' workshops often pull together basic rules of literature and journalism and provide an atmosphere where writers compose on-the-spot articles, short stories, or novels. Workshops are intensive; they often last at least a day or a weekend. Some, like the annual Dixie Council of Authors and Journalists workshop, last a week. The Council meets each spring at St. Simons Island on the Georgia coast, attracting writers from eastern seaboard states as well as a few from as far away as California and Alaska. (For details, write novelist Frances Statham, 2248 Marann Dr., Atlanta GA 30345.)

Workshops like these thoroughly immerse participants in writing. They dine with other writers, study together, criticize one another's work, chat about writing during coffee breaks, and fall asleep to the tapping of the writer's keyboard in the room next door.

Veteran writer, editor, and workshop instructor Bill

25 Alphabets, Books, Courses

Emerson once enchanted over one hundred writers for three days at the 1981 *Reader's Digest*/University of South Carolina writer's workshop (for information contact *Reader's Digest* in Pleasantville, New York.)

"Getting away from home to a writer's workshop is like sticking your head into a bowl of fudge," Emerson says. "You lick up information and inspiration at a writers' workshop and come away with a taste for the profession you could never get from poking yourself into a course at the local college for an hour a week. Being at a writer's workshop is eating and breathing and living your writing. Nobody I know ever died of an overdose."

Every year, at least two hundred writers' conferences or workshops are held across the United States. They fall into several categories: specific (about a certain form of writing, such as poetry or writing for a religious audience); general fiction or nonfiction; beginning or advanced (the advanced workshops are usually for published professionals); book, magazine, or newspaper writing.

If you can afford it, sample all categories, no matter what your specific interest may be. A short story writer can learn a lot from a journalism workshop, for instance, because it will teach him brevity of style. Prices for workshops vary from about $50 to $250 for several daylong sessions, depending on the number of days attended and who the instructors are. Be sure to take travel, food, and lodging costs into consideration. Find out if scholarships are available; some university workshops may reduce prices for worthy potential students, while private workshops may be sponsored by scholarship-granting foundations.

If you want personal attention, find out if workshop classes are limited in enrollment. Ten students are often the most an instructor allows if he hopes to spend meaningful time with each one. To find out where and when writers' workshops are being held, look in local newspapers, *Publishers Weekly*, the *Lit-*

erary *Market Place*, and *Writer's Digest* magazine. You can subscribe to these periodicals or get copies at your local library. The May 1982 issue of *Writer's Digest* lists more than two hundred workshops with the names and addresses of people to contact. If a workshop you like has already been held this year, write about plans for next year and ask if any others will be on the calendar soon.

Workshops are a good way to make friends and acquire business contacts, too. And, if you do get to a workshop or two, the knowledge you acquire and the new buddies you meet will combine as a worthwhile investment.

USE CRITICISM SERVICES

Writers also learn from constructive criticism offered by many reading and criticism services, some of which are run by solitary writers who work from their homes. A skillful teacher functions as your best critic, and so do objective writers who may read your work as a favor. Don't hand over manuscripts to friends or relatives; as a rule, they have a hard time being objective.

The *West Coast Review of Books* will accept and review unpublished manuscripts; several novels have been bought by publishers who read good reviews in its pages. The reviews also serve as constructive criticism for new writers. To be reviewed, send a copy of your novel, fastened in a binder, to the magazine at 6565 Sunset Blvd., Hollywood CA 90028.

Writer's Digest has a criticism service, and there are many others which advertise in writers' magazines and at workshops. Employ services that promise only to review your work and send you a written comment. Be wary of possible "sharks" who want fat fees and trumpet a guarantee of publication. The costs for criticism services vary widely. Decide how much an objective opinion is worth, and get a list in writing of what the service entails *before* you fork over a penny.

* * *

Other writers can help with constructive criticism, says novelist and book critic Tom Cook. His first novel, *Blood Innocence*, was nominated for the Edgar Allan Poe Award of the Mystery Writers of America. Cook's nomination gave him the confidence to begin several other novels, and he now writes two at one time; one he calls "literary" and the other, "an easy detective story."

As he weaves back and forth between these two types of books, devoting a morning to one and an afternoon to the other, Cook finds it helpful to have the observations and advice of other writers who will comment on his work. But it's neither polite nor practical to interrupt a friend's dinner or workday to ask him to read your latest chapter. So Cook helped form a writers' group, which meets twice a month in his book-stuffed living room. He says such groups are a substitute or adjunct to a private teacher or class, and they can be an invaluable educational tool.

There may be a flourishing writers' group in your community. If not, here's the proper way, says Cook, to form and use such a group:

"Invite only people who see their futures in terms of writing. They don't all have to be writers; it may be good to include one or two future critics or a person who is in some way deeply involved in reading all the time, such as the manager of a good local bookstore. But they should all be professionals. Remove the diddlers. And stay away from people who indicate that they're writing as a substitute for going to a psychotherapist.

"Keep the membership to a maximum of ten people. Only three or four, at the most, will be able to read their work at each meeting. Meet once every two weeks.

"From time to time you may want to invite a guest—say, a respected local editor—but try to keep people from fluttering in and out. You want stability.

"Mix the talent, so you have one person writing a comedy, one a mystery, and so on. But no poets. Novelists and poets don't mix; the form is too different. And you want people who know enough about form to correct yours.

"Pledge everyone to honesty. When they don't like something they should tell you why, and how to make it better. No hostility, of course. But when you're writing fiction the last thing you need is insincere flattery.

"Keep writing and reading as you attend the group."

The Writer's Community, a New York group, also uses peer criticism as a learning tool. It has set up meetings for fiction writers who want others to hear and comment on their manuscripts. You can attend ten sessions for twenty-five dollars. To apply, send a manuscript, résumé, and self-addressed, stamped envelope to The Studio, c/o the Writer's Community, 120 E. Eighty-ninth St., New York NY 10028. The telephone number is (202)628-0239.

You can educate yourself, insists Truman Capote. He says he ignored his formal education in favor of analyzing short stories and novels on his own, constantly struggling to perfect his technique as he went along. By the time he stunned the world with *In Cold Blood* in 1965, he had taught himself the new style later called "faction." This was characterized by an artful blending of journalism with crawl-into-the-mind-of-the-character dramatization. Capote didn't copy the style from anybody else; he developed it through constant trial and error, and by careful attention to the basics of his craft. Formal schooling, he claims, played little or no part in his development as a writer.

"I never did any homework [as a child]," Capote told an interviewer for *Vogue* magazine in December 1979. "My literary tasks kept me fully occupied: my apprenticeship at the altar of technique; craft; the devilish intricacies of paragraphing, punctuation, dialogue placement. Not to mention the grand overall design, the great demanding arc of beginning-middle-end. One had to learn so much, and from so many sources: not only from books, but from music, from painting, and, to be sure, just plain everyday observation."

Observe life, advises novelist, short story writer, book reviewer and writing teacher Paul Darcy Boles. Recognized as one of the great masters of American fiction, Boles has been writing and selling fiction since he was a teenager. He warns that no matter what writing courses you take, they cannot help unless you train youself to be a careful observer of life's details.

"You must be aware of the constant process of discovery when you are learning about writing and when you are actually doing it. The most important thing you can do is to learn about life and human nature, life and its tremendous possibilities. Don't think of how much money you can make, at least not at first. Instead, work on doing the best you can. *Then* you might make some money. Look at the weight of emotion or sheer information each sentence carries. You must learn to be patient enough to go over your work sentence by sentence. It won't do much good if you observe life carefully and don't observe your own writng about it."

Observe yourself, says writer and editor Chuck Lawliss, who spent $300 and three half-days on aptitude testing to see if fiction was his future. Lawliss reported on aptitude testing in the June 26, 1981, issue of *Publishers Weekly*, after going through the tests at the Human Engineering Laboratory of the Johnson O'Connor Research Foundation at 11 E. Sixty-second Street in New York City.

Lawliss said he found that aptitudes are natural talents. They are apparently special—and perhaps inborn—abilities for learning to do certain things. Aptitudes become part of a person "like the color of one's eyes." Knowledge, on the other hand, is acquired. Knowledge is needed to use aptitudes effectively. Aptitudes suggest the direction your writing should go in; knowledge helps you get there. "Fiction might be recommended over nonfiction, criticism over exposition. Even promising subject areas may be suggested and whether a large or small publishing house might be the better bet . . . " said Lawliss. He claims that the testing taught him that editors tend to score lower in foresight, remarkably high in analytical reasoning and very well in language abilities. Science fiction writers, said Lawliss, score high in structural thinking. "I was surprised to learn that successful people in every line of endeavor share one thing in common, and often only one: a large vocabulary," he added. Lawliss made it clear that aptitude testing isn't for everyone. But it can be helpful for writers who are confused about which way to guide their careers, or for those who feel insecure about their choice of writing as a way of life.

Reading is the best education, says novelist Stuart Woods. He agrees with critic/writer Vermont Royster, who declares flatly, "As for writing skill, in no way can it be taught to those who do not read." Woods's first novel, *Chiefs*, was an instant success in 1981 and was made into a six-hour television series. He feels that reading was the single most important factor in establishing himself as a novelist.

"My mother taught me to read a year before I started elementary school. I've clamored for books ever since. She read *Lassie Come Home* to me and in the middle of the book she handed it to me and said, 'Here, read the rest yourself.' I was six years old and I had to find out what happened to that poor old dog, so I got through the book on my own . . . I credit a healthy appetite for books with training myself to write novels. My best advice to other authors is to read. Read everything. Read a lot!"

31 Alphabets, Books, Courses

Read as a writer, says R.V. Cassill, who had made a career out of that advice. He is the author of several novels, a fiction teacher at Brown University, and a former fiction workshop leader for *Writer's Digest*. In his *Norton Anthology of Short Fiction*, Cassill reviews eighty-seven works of ficton from authors as diverse as Herman Melville, Virginia Woolf, and Joyce Carol Oates. To Cassill, reading and analyzing fiction is essential for a writer, and serves as the fiction writer's best education.

"When you read, make notes in the margins. Don't just underline; you may forget why you underlined that passage. Describe how the passage struck you and how you would use it in your own story. Note the *concept* of the story, and then figure out how the trained writer fulfilled it by his *mechanics*. Pay attention to the use of dialogue, descriptions of scenes, character development, and creative use of punctuation. In this way you will learn to use good writers as your models.

"Part of your training as a writer should be to copy excellent passages from a master's novel. This will teach you rhythm, style, and punctuation.

"When reading magazine short stories, you may want to clip out passages that thrill you. Paste the clipping on a page in a special notebook, and under that write down what you like about that passage. Then, immediately try to transfer it to a story of your own."

Read to write better, asserts Felix Stefanile, a professor of English at Purdue University and editor at Sparrow Press. In an essay in *The New York Times Book Review*, Stefanile advises beginning authors to read something good, and then take a break—go for a walk or have a beer—to give their minds a chance to digest and analyze what they've read.

"What else is there to say? Read. Writers read. Writers always read, though not all writers admit this. Reading is the writer's, the editor's, way of staying in touch, of keeping ready, of being alert. Read for the love of it, for the fun, and for the challenge. Read, and for heaven's sake, buy a book once in a while and support the other fellow."

2 | Tools of the Trade

I STARTED THIS CHAPTER with a Flair pen and a Sparco legal pad. I finished on a sleek computer that transformed my office and my writing habits forever.

For some writers, it's cheap to set up shop. I once figured a few sharp pencils and a stack of paper would do the job. For years, it did. I even made friends with the manager of a local office supply store, who let me buy inexpensive, slightly imperfect lined paper for first drafts.

But scratching out plots in longhand became tedious and time-consuming. It was easier to find something else to do, like washing dishes. One day I realized I had a dishwasher for that chore in my kitchen, but there was very little in my office upstairs to ease the tedium of getting thoughts on paper.

That day, I forced myself to write directly on the typewriter instead of putting stories down in longhand, then editing and typing. I have a portable, $130 Smith-Corona Coronet Electric # 10 typewriter that has served my family well for almost a decade. In a pinch, it fulfills the major requirements of an editor: clean, easy-to-read copy, double-spaced, using pica (not elite or script) type.

Soon I wanted something more. First I looked for a typewriter with automatic erasing. These are a step up, and usually cost at least fifty dollars more than non-erasing electric typewriters. If you want one, be sure to test the correction system, because many of these typewriters "white out" mistakes rather than "lift off" the image from the page. The "white out" leaves a blotch on your paper.

GOOD TOOLS ARE A "MUST"

If you're going to submit your work for sale, there's no getting around the need for a good writing tool. It may be a manual typewriter, an electric typewriter, an electronic typewriter, or a word processor. To be good it must produce a sharp image, not skip spaces, and make typing as easy as possible.

You'll probably need at least an electric typewriter (or a very good manual) and new ribbons. You should use quality bond paper for final drafts, and it's a good idea to have professional-looking letterhead stationery for typed cover letters to editors. Don't believe the snobbish boasts of writers who say they do all right with cranky typewriters or scribbled notes to the editor on folded brown grocery bags. Editors won't plow through sloppy manuscripts, and none will accept handwritten work. Maybe Ernest Hemingway's editor put up with penciled notes, but I don't know any writers who get away with less than a good-looking typed manuscript and cover letter.

You must invest in a typewriter unless you're going to hire a secretary or a typing service. I don't recommend either. Secretaries are expensive, and typing services often farm a book out to several different people. The result may be several different interpretations of your work and the grim possibility of several varieties of typographical mistakes.

If you need a manuscript typed and can't afford a typewriter right now, try renting one. Also ask if a shop will sell you a good used brand at a reduced price. If you must have someone else type the work for you, be sure that the person has a good typewriter and understands exactly how you want the completed manuscript to look.

An electric typewriter is usually the first major investment a writer can afford. If work piles up and you can afford to pay more, investigate electronic typewriters. They speed the writing process and may have a small "memory bank," which allows you to press a button and let the machine (not you) retype a brief letter or story. Electronic typewriters can cost from one to three thousand dollars. There is an excellent description and comparison of several brands of electronic or "smart" typewriters in the April 1982 issue of *Writer's Digest* magazine.

WHAT ABOUT WORD PROCESSORS?

The most sophisticated writer's aid these days is a word processor. The major advantage of this machine is that its TV-like screen or line window shows the page before it's typed. The operator can quickly change words, insert or delete paragraphs, erase, and edit on the screen or window. Nothing goes on paper until the page is perfected. Then, press a button to command the processor, and the page is swiftly typed. On the better processors (about seven thousand dollars) the page will be so perfectly done that it appears to be printed. You can store many pages on discs resembling records and easily revise and make copies of your work.

That's a simplification of word processors; you need at least a full day of intensive instruction to find out what they can really do. The company from which you buy the processor should supply you with free in-house training on your machine or on one exactly like it. And you should have the services of a trainer for several hours at your home after you buy the machine, in addition to unlimited telephone assistance if you get confused.

It's important to buy a word processor from a company

with a good reputation for service. The machine is useless unless it's backed by experts who know how to use it, how to teach *you* to use it, and how to fix it. I started my adventure with word processors by lugging home a used Lanier. When it broke down too often and I got fed up, the company went to great lengths to supply me with free back-up tools, and eventually offered a healthy discount on a new machine. If you do buy a word processor, new or used, be sure that it's backed by a firm that will spring to your aid if things go wrong. Ask for use of the machine, free, for a least two weeks before you decide to buy. If it breaks down, a serviceperson should be at your home within eight hours. You might want to rent or lease the processor to see if it works well for you. You can always buy it later.

Spend as much time as possible investigating newspaper ads and nosing around office supply stores before you buy any writing tool. I was fortunate in having the help of novelist Stuart Woods and computer specialist Mark Sutherland, two friends who helped me with comparison shopping. Stuart lent me his printer, and Mark hooked it up to a used word processor. They puffed up two flights of stairs to my office and hooked up the heavy components, then were kind enough to puff downstairs again a week later when I decided I didn't like that setup. Later, Mark helped me settle on another, less cumbersome machine.

If you don't have friends who use the machine you are investigating and can offer advice about it, it may pay to hire an objective specialist to go shopping with you. Ask office supply stores to give you the names of several freelance equipment specialists who might perform this service for an hourly fee. It's better to spend fifty dollars for good advice than waste several hundred dollars, or more, because you made a mistake on the wrong tool.

START WITH SIMPLE TOOLS

Fancy typewriters and word processors are marvelous writing aids because they speed the creative process for some people and eliminate the drudgery. But I recommend them only if you're a career writer. They're expensive, and they mean a permanent change in work habits. Until you're ready, simpler and less expensive equipment will see you through: a dictionary, thesaurus, pen or pencil, lined paper for handwritten first drafts, good unlined paper for final drafts, and a typewriter with a clean ribbon. Some fine writers, in fact, snicker at sophisticated toools because they say machines impede the flow of creative juices. Spy novelist John le Carre, author of *Smiley's People* and other thrillers, uses only felt-tipped Pentels. Novelist Pat Conroy scratched out *The Lords of Discipline* in longhand, because he loathes even typewriters.

COUNT YOUR COSTS

No matter what you use, remember to deduct any writing tools from your income taxes. Tad Crawford's *Writer's Legal Guide* will give you information on how to claim deductions. Keep all expense receipts; tally up the money you spend on everything from phone calls to typewriter ribbon. Writing is a business, and you should keep business-like files on all income and expenses.

BUILD YOUR OWN "TOOL CHEST"

According to a recent natonal survey, the most important writing tools are tape recorders, typewriters, and telephones. Fiction writers use tape recorders to capture the flavor of a character's speech and to "talk out" their thoughts before they write. Telephones are vital long-distance links with sources of information, agents and editors.

To me, books are also important writer's aids. Nonfiction

books give critical information on writing and research. Fiction books can be analyzed for technique and used for inspiration. Magazines also spark ideas and provide information. Facts are gleaned from newspapers; good newspaper feature stories, like those found on the front page of *The Wall Street Journal*, provide ideas for fiction and writing hints.

You also need a comfortable table and chair, a quiet, pleasant place to work, and a steaming pot of good coffee.

Actually, a "tool" is anything that helps you write. That includes trade magazines, writers' workshops, a comfortable chair, or the network of contact people you cultivated for information or ideas. In this chapter writers talk about the tools they use so you can glean ideas and have some basis of comparison. But remember: you must build a "tool chest" of your own. It may not work for anyone else, but that doesn't matter. Collect only the tools that make writing easier for *you*. Anything else is a toy. Throw it away.

* * *

Never throw away anything you can use for reference material for novel writing, advises Lawrence Block. He has written two nonfiction books and over one hundred novels, and tells the readers of his monthly column that he keeps regional books, maps, and travel guides so he can have his characters speak with authority about various parts of the country or the world.

"I also keep an atlas close at hand, and my filing cabinet contains a sheaf of maps of all sorts—road maps, city maps, everything. I hang on to guidebooks, too. I have a slightly out-of-date set of Mobil Travel Guides and a variety of individual guides for foreign countries and various sections of this country. Sometimes I'll set a book or part of a book in a region with which I'm unfamiliar, and I want to be able to provide a couple of specific touches to make the background convincing. A good geographic library not only helps me to appear knowledgeable but also helps stimulate the fiction factory in my head."

Stimulate your fiction factory with photographs. That's the advice of actor/writer Roy Sorrels. When he taught acting at Long Beach State College, Sorrels wrote, he instructed his students to clip dramatic photos from newspapers and magazines to study the characters in them. Then, the students would "crawl into the skins" of the people in the photos, acting out scenes from their fictional lives. It works for writers, too, Sorells says. The reality of the photograph triggers your imagination, providing a springboard for action.

Seeing a real person in a real environment, said Sorrels, makes the writer start talking about that person, feeling his emotions, and even trying to enter his mind. "Get her [you!] talking about the smells, textures, sounds, sights, tastes of that world. It's the most exciting kind of trip there is; it's the trip you want your readers to experience, and you must show the way."

Tape precise dialogue as a way of capturing characters, suggests novelist Anne Rivers Siddons. The latest of her several novels is *Fox's Earth*, a thriller about an evil woman of the South. In this book, the main character's voice is an echo of the often-wicked Southern past; Siddons was able to keep that voice constant by employing her tape recorder as a tool.

"I use my tape recorder to capture the precise flavor of dialects around the South, and to record language that soon may not exist any more. I often take the recorder with me in the car, and perhaps if I play it the character will come clear to me while I'm driving. It helps a lot to 'hear' my character speak this way. Her voice becomes real to me."

Reality is a tool for Celestine Sibley, a novelist, short story writer, reporter, and columnist for the *Atlanta Constitution*. Her most recent novel, *Children, My Children*, is painfully realistic in its simple details about a grandmother's search for her lost offspring. It illustrates Sibley's commitment to everyday items as tools of the writer.

"I could get very simple about it all and write fiction in longhand, but I've been a reporter so long that I can't *think* in longhand anymore. I wouldn't mind a word processor, but, well, when I get up to write at 3:00 a.m., I'm doing well just to plug in my coffee percolator.

"My Royal typewriter is so old, it could have been used to write *Pilgrim's Progress*. But it turns out a neat job. I'd like a new one, maybe an electric, but I'd rather spend a thousand dollars on my grandchildren's education than on a new writing tool for myself.

"Weird things from real life are my tools. The picture from an old calendar might give me an idea for the way a country kitchen should look. The name on the back of a boat in my novel came from a friend's name for her business.

"Aside from those common things, my other basic tools are *Webster's New World Dictionary*, John Bartlett's *Familiar Quotations*, and *Brewer's Dictionary of Phrase and Fable*. They are the only books I keep on my desk at all times."

Books are the best tools for Arthur Hailey, author of bestselling novels *Airport*, *Hotel* and *Wheels*. Hailey feels that his writing would suffer without the use of good books, so he keeps favorites nearby like *The Synonym Finder* from Rodale Books and *The Comprehensive Word Guide* by Norman Lewis.

"No matter how good one's vocabulary, there is often a 'better word' if you take the trouble to look for it. The *New York Times Manual of Style and Usage* is an excellent, concise arbiter of grammatical and style queries. I also use the *Dictionary of Amer-*

ican Slang by Wentworth and Flexner. It's hard to keep up-to-date, though. I have my children read passages using slang; they often revise them."

Revise easily on a word processor, says novelist Robin Perry.

He has been investigating the machines for six years and uses an Olivetti TES 401. Perry maintains that word processors encourage a writer to revise as often as necessary, thus improving his work.

"There is a big difference between a story written, edited, and typed by hand and one that is worked over *as many times as necessary* to wring every last bit of creativity out of the prose. I am often asked how I can justify spending eight thousand dollars on a writing tool. Well, an electrician or plumber wouldn't think twice about spending the same amount of money for a truck for his business. If your business is writing, as mine is, the expense is reasonable."

A writer's expenses can spiral, says magazine and book writer James Lincoln Collier.

Authors may not realize how poorly they're paid until they add up the costs of their tools. In an article for the July 31, 1981, issue of *Publishers Weekly,* Collier lamented that writers may not be able to afford the tools of their trade unless publishers come across with more money.

"It has been said that a writer needs nothing but a typewriter and a ream of paper in order to work. Unfortunately, this is not the truth. A professional writer runs a small business and has all the expenses of any small businessperson: rent; utilities; heat; secretarial services; phone; mailing; lawyers' and accountants' fees; as well as research expenses such as travel and books that other small businesspeople don't have. Another expense that other small businesspeople don't have is the agent's fee, which is also ten percent, sometimes fifteen percent."

Movies are valuable for adventure novelist Bill Diehl, who struck it rich when his first novel, *Sharkey's Machine*, was filmed by actor Burt Reynolds. Diehl says he now thinks about a movie treatment when he writes, using movies to give him inspiration for scenes he wants to portray in his books.

"I watch a lot of movies. I have a waist-high stack of film cassettes in my bedroom, and I run off a film either to inspire a scene or to perfect it in my mind.

"I have a lot of other tools, too. I use a word processor. It dominates my home office, and lets me write and edit virtually at the same moment. It projects my writing on a screen, and that's natural to me because I'm a screen-type person.

"I have a telephone answering device which I turn on while I'm writing. It takes calls so I don't have to stop and answer the phone.

"I also have a good, big Xerox machine. I make copies of my work for my agent, my editor, and for friends I really trust. You could say friends are a writing tool for me. I send my work to friends who read a lot and who can react to what I write in various ways, either emotionally or technically, or as an overview. One of my friends was able to nail three things that were wrong with my most recent novel, *Chameleon*. That helped me revise a couple of extremely important points.

"It's fun to have the help of friends. It's fun to use my tools, especially the movies. If something isn't fun, I don't use it."

3 | Finding Good Fiction Ideas

FOR A WRITER, terror is facing an empty page with no idea of how to fill it up.

It happens a lot, even to professionals. World-famous Russian author Alexsandr Solzhenitsyn once told a reporter he was almost glad when police dragged him off to a Soviet labor camp, because being in prison gave him a lot of story ideas.

"Before I was arrested," he said, "I just felt depressed because it was so difficult, I thought, to find fresh subjects for stories."

A SLICE OF LIFE

Story subjects come from life experiences. Things happen to you—and to other people—that somehow clang a bell in your mind and make you gasp, "Isn't *that* odd?" or "What if that had happened to me?"

Sooner or later most writers learn the "isn't that" or "what if" game. They become experts at viewing everyday events and expanding on them by imagining other events that could follow.

It isn't necessary to toil in a slave labor camp to find story ideas. Those ideas can come from watching a child grimace at the sound of his mother's call, or listening to a bawdy street fight among neighbors. If the event illuminates some small part of human nature, it might make a good short story. If there's a long history around the event, it's probably a novel. Sometimes there is no way to tell what form the event will take in your writing or how it will expand until you begin putting words on paper.

FICTION FROM FACT

I find many fiction ideas while I'm researching factual articles. To me, real events are exciting. It takes just a little shove of imagination, a little tugging at the truth here and there, to turn fact into fiction.

I once watched a gorilla suckle her newborn in a primate research laboratory. I was then doing a magazine article on the mothering instincts of the great apes. The scientist in charge told me a funny story about how that particular gorilla once grabbed him affectionately and almost crushed his ribs in a well-meaning hug.

"Maybe she's in love with me," the scientist chuckled. "That happens, you know. Gorillas have often tried to behave like lovers toward the people who take care of them." Then he added with a comical sigh, "She *is* sweet. She gives me more affection than some humans I know."

I went home and started *Darby's Gorilla*, a book about a primate specialist who left his wife because he "went ape" over a female gorilla. Later, a visit to a state hospital for retarded children spawned *Notes From Another World*, a story about a little girl who was left to "rot" in an institution because her mother didn't want to take care of her. A friend who showed courage in the face of illness and divorce inspired another novel, *Wounded Birds*.

Other writers also pluck ideas from places they visit and people they know, weaving parts of their own lives into the fabric of the story. Novelist Stuart Woods trembled through the death of two close friends; his second book is about a man whose life is changed when two friends die. Celestine Sibley, who writes novels and newspaper columns, is a devoted grandmother. She put a lot of her own fears into a novel about the disappearance of a woman's grandchildren. Novelist Terry Kay grew up in the country and heard a lot of stories about the harsh life of rural Southerners. Many of those same stories are in his novel, *After Eli*.

Some writing evolves from what the pros call "formula ideas." A few of these come straight from the Bible; a twist on the story of Adam and Eve, when a woman causes a man's downfall (or the other way around); a takeoff on the story of Ruth, a devoted woman (or man, or child, or even an animal) who becomes attached to a person's family or cause in life after the person dies; or a variation of the saga of Moses, the poor kid who becomes a rich kid quite by accident, then sadly renounces his foster family to help those he left behind. Good modern stories are also based on other classics. *West Side Story*, for example, is a takeoff on *Romeo and Juliet*. There's probably no end to how you could vary and update *Hamlet*, *Macbeth*, and other timeless works. Such stories can be set in any place, at any time. They've captured the imagination of readers and kept it this long because the themes are eternal.

Recently, new formula ideas have been successful. There are novels or short stories about the woman who struggles for liberation; people who cope with modern problems such as divorce, drugs, meaningless sex, stepparenting, or disrespect for old age; and any good treatment of the terrors of living with teenagers.

FAMILIAR THEMES

Don't worry if the themes sound too familiar. A good idea is a new slant on an old subject. The best story ideas, in fact, are often familiar enough to be instantly recognizable. Your reader should be able to say, "Gee, this could happen to me," or "I know someone like that!" Even if the story idea is "wild," as it may be in science fiction, the inclusion of familiar details and down-home human emotions will allow the reader to suspend disbelief. He'll forget he's reading a story, getting so wound up in your characters' lives that he momentarily thinks they are real.

Most of all, the idea must be real to *you*. It probably won't come fast; ideas usually don't flash before you like bursts of divine light. They ripen slowly. Be patient. You may find that the idea you had for a short story gradually expands into a novel, or suddenly loses its glitter on page two. Don't lock yourself into preset notions of how or when you should produce ideas, or what you should do with them when they do come.

The only meaningful ritual that surrounds almost every writer's ideas is to carefully jot them down in a notebook set aside for the purpose. Good ideas may come at the most inappropriate times—when you're jogging, in the shower, or mowing the lawn—and you must train yourself to stop what you are doing and get them on paper before they are lost.

As for the rest of it, you will find that experience is your best guide in finding ways to come up with ideas and turn them into salable fiction.

Life experiences provide a warehouse of story ideas, according to Celestine Sibley. She has become nationally known through her syndicated tales of ordinary people and their daily joys and tragedies; she reminds us that the best ideas come from the little things in life.

"I've got lots of different kinds of friends. I know alcoholics, beggars, ladies of the night, farmers, hardworking folks with grease under their fingernails, all the way up to Rosalynn Carter and everyone in between. I've been out on all kinds of crazy newspaper stories, in a tornado, with houses blowing down all around me; and in a house with the mother of an escaped convict, while the convict was hiding in a closet right behind me. This adds up to a lot of life experience, and I think that's the best thing a writer can have. You learn that living is made up of little things, like drying a child's tears and being glad when your pie comes out of the oven, filling the kitchen with sweetness. I prefer stories that revolve around human emotions we all share. The best ideas involve just plain people. You don't have to write about the big shots or famous persons. The policeman on the corner or the beggar on the street probably both have better stories."

Markets influence the flow of ideas, according to Lawrence Block. In his book, *Writing the Novel from Plot to Print*, Block notes that today's writers often think "novel" instead of "short story" because there's more of a market for novels. That affects the way ideas take shape.

"Each short story absolutely demands either a new idea or a fresh slant on an old one. Novels don't demand this. They can just be good page-turners. If you've decided that money is the spur that goads you and that you want to reach for the brass ring right away rather than work your way up to it, you would do well to have a broad acquaintance with the sorts of books that have made authors rich. By regularly reading bestselling novels, and especially by concentrating on the works of those authors who consistently hit the bestseller list, you'll develop a sense of the sorts of books which tend to earn big money."

Developing ideas can be a painful process, admits Lois Duncan, who writes nonfiction, short stories, and novels for children and young adults. From her home in Albuquerque, New Mexico, Duncan scans newspapers, other books, and anything she can find for story ideas.

"My most recent novel is *Stranger With My Face*; that idea came when I was looking in the mirror, and the thought popped into my head, 'What if I saw my reflection smile back at me . . . but I wasn't smiling? How could that happen?' That started the painful process of figuring out how the thing could happen, how the idea could materialize.

"The process can only begin when I'm ready. That's when I *need* to do a book. I try to do one a year, and balance the subjects so I don't follow a book with one that's too much like it.

"When I know the need is there, I go shopping for my idea. At this moment I know I want a subject for a youth novel that's a thriller. My mind becomes open because I'm ready to find an idea. An idea may have passed me by while I was doing something else, but I didn't see it because I was preoccupied; I wasn't ready.

"I read a little piece in the newspapers about a boy who came back alone from a camping trip, and he couldn't tell anyone what happened to his young partner. That set me off. I started wondering, 'What could have happened to the other boy?' And from there I started thinking of all the things that could have happened—all scary—and the idea began to take shape.

"It's an intricate and painful process. You get the idea, but that's just the first step. It leads to more and more questions. You have to ask, 'What viewpoint should it be written from? Should it be done in first person? Who is my reader; how old should he or she be? How old is my character going to be, and what are his life circumstances?'

"Each step, each decision, advances the idea. It's hard, it's time-consuming, it's sometimes confusing, and always painful. But it has to be done."

Popular ideas are often married to form, declares historical romance writer Frances Statham. Several years ago she read a "mushy" paperback and decided to do one of her own as a lark. She turned out a novel sitting in a car, waiting to pick her children up from school, and it sold at once. Now she gets huge advances for her historical romance sagas and says if you know the form a certain type of book is supposed to take, you can quickly get ideas.

"For me the question is, 'Am I writing a Gothic or a historical romance?' A Gothic really has no sex. It's a sweet murder mystery. You have a young heroine coming to a dark house, presided over by a handsome master. He limps. He has a lunatic wife hidden in the attic. He falls in love with the heroine. The heroine is afraid, but madly attracted to the master. Fate pulls them apart, but in the end they fall into one another's arms. The wife dies with a smile on her lips.

"In the historical romance there's an initial encounter with a hero, then the lovely lady is separated from him and forced to have sex with other men. They are all brutes. The two lovers find each other in the end. I've done a little twist on these forms by keeping my lovers together, and allowing the heroine to escape the violent beds of other men. But basically the form dictates my story, and that makes it easy to get ideas.

Nonfiction articles spur novel ideas. Reporter Robert Coram did research on drug smuggling for a series of newspaper and magazine articles and decided to turn his information into a novel. To avoid revealing inside information, he changed names, dates, and places and fictionalized his characters.

"I can weave some pretty hot information on drug smuggling into a novel without compromising my sources. For instance, I found out that the Russians are involved in drug smuggling in this country. It's a good way for them to make money, and they're happy to get Americans doped up. I couldn't spill this in nonfiction—not yet—without getting into hot water. But I sure can use it in a novel.

"There's a nonfiction book here, and I am going to do it someday. But right now, fiction gives me more latitude. It boils down to this: I want to do a novel. A lot of the time you have to fictionalize ideas simply because you *want* to."

Real events turn into fiction. On the day Elvis Presley died, Gail Brewer-Giorgio began a novel about a rock singer imprisoned by his own fame. She finished *Orion* in fifty-four days, found a publisher, and began negotiating movie rights.

"It wasn't until people read my book and said, 'This is about Elvis Presley, isn't it?' that I realized how closely my story paralleled reality.

"I was never a rabid Presley fan. It wasn't his life that gave me the idea for a novel, but his death. I remember sitting in my living room, listening to the news about how he died, and feeling very sorry for what the world had done to him. He was a prisoner of his own popularity and success, and to be free he had to die. I thought, 'Suppose he isn't really dead? Suppose he faked his own death as a way of being free to start a new, more normal life?'

"It was a nifty idea. I sat down and wrote it."

Nifty ideas don't always work. Edward Keyes should know; one of his ideas for a novel fizzled out soon after he began writing. Keyes had already worked on a novel with another author, which became *The French Connection*, a successful movie. But he told *Publishers Weekly* that when he tried again, on his own, he got into trouble because he didn't know enough about his subject. He abandoned the idea, started anew, and was successful writing about a subject with which he was familiar.

Keyes said his first book was a great idea, but it failed because "I really didnt' know what it was about." He got about one third into the book and developed massive writer's block; work just stopped. He says he had no feel for where he was going and his own words seemed alien. Ultimately he had to give the money for his advance back to the publisher. Later, he wrote about another hero: an educated man in the restaurant business. This was a character with which Keys was more familiar. Keyes really knew all the things that could happen because he knew the protagonist and the federal officers that made him turn informer. His new work was based on reality, Keyes said, so the book could go forward. His experience is a lesson to all writers: stick with what you know. If you can't *feel* the material, and your subject holds no real fascination for you, you're probably on the wrong track.

Use newspapers to find more "blueprints," suggests R.V. Cassill. If you know how to elaborate on what's going on in the world, Cassill says, you'll find a wealth of story ideas every day on the front page of your local newspaper.

"Remember the Scarsdale murder? What a story idea! A wealthy doctor spurns his middle-aged lover. She finds him in the arms of a younger woman. So she shoots him and walks off to jail with her nose in the air.

"That story provides any novelist with a super plot and entrancing characters. You can use it almost as is, or do a take-off on the concept of the spurned older woman.

"If you use newspapers to find story ideas you'll never have to ask yourself, 'Could this really happen?' You know it did."

Idea isn't as important as craft, insists William Winn, who writes and studies short stories, and selects and edits them for *ATLANTA* magazine. (He once read 600 short stories in one week.) What goes wrong with most fiction is not weakness of the idea, Winn believes, but of the writer's ability to carry it out.

"I see so much contemporary fiction mauled by writers who don't study the craft before they sit down and attempt to write. I can tell in the first five lines if the sentence structure and style is that of a person who hasn't done his homework.

"These are writers with no literary education, no general fund of knowledge about the writers who came before them. Instead of reading other fine work, studying it, taking it apart, going into the history of literature, they're trying to write sentiment off the tops of their heads.

"Lack of study results in lack of a deep system of values. That shows up in the fiction. And lack of study also spotlights a writer who doesn't have what I call 'word-sense.' That means he doesn't know that words have different shapes, different forms. A good writer knows the weight of a word, and partly through study, partly through inborn talent, he picks just the right one.

"It's not the idea that goes wrong. It's all the other things, mostly brought about because the writer is too lazy to study literature before he tries to produce it."

Ideas boil up in desperation, says bestselling novelist Frederick Forsyth. Inspiration for *The Day of the Jackal*, Forsyth told a reporter, came after he was fired from his job in 1970 and needed money to stay afloat. He used his knowledge of international affairs to write the thriller, which was rejected four times before he finally found a publisher.

"It took me about six weeks on a battered typewriter. I never dreamed it would become what it became. Current events moved the concept along, but the idea of writing a novel came in the first place because I needed money."

Love inspires great fiction ideas, declares world-famous actor and writer David Niven. Love stories—yours and others'—spur thoughts about what happens to lovers when fate parts them or puts obstacles in their path. Add your own experiences, says Niven, and you've got the idea for a novel. Niven wrote two memoirs before starting on his first novel, *Go Slowly, Come Back Quickly*.

"It's about young people in love in turbulent times, during World War II. It's really a simple love story with lots of fresh air. I was part of practically everything I describe in it, so I didn't have to do much research. My idea was simply to write about two attractive young people in love, and include a lot of outdoor action. The fresh air idea again, you see, and I did't use an outline. If I have any advice for other writers, it's not to worry too much about how clever an idea might be. Story ideas don't have to knock the reader out of his chair. The action will do that.

"Just take your characters out of their stuffy houses and put them in action in the great outdoors."

4 | Riches from Research

RESEARCH IS THE SOUL of writing. It's the writer's way of educating himself, building a solid foundation for his fiction, and having fun at the same time. Editors warm to writers who are careful reporters, too, and when they find a writer who won't do research, they consider him lazy.

You need research on history, location, dress, mannerisms, and social mores to pump authenticity into your novels and short stories. Dates, times, accurate descriptions of places—even correct snatches of song—all lend weight to your words. Professional writers spend considerable time on research. It's the amateurs who prefer to philosophize about life, to pen essays on personal ideals. Such work rarely sells.

Many professionals start with market research. Before they begin to write, they may contact publishers to find out what types of books are selling best. Then they construct a story to fit current market needs. Larry Ashmead, a senior editor at Harper & Row, says most books are now bought by women. So novels, for, by, and about women are usually the most successful.

FACT SHEETS ON FICTION

Getting information like that is the most basic form of research. Many publishers put out fact sheets, listing their primary markets (who buys their books); their favorite subjects (what to write about); and the most successful style (how to write it). The fact sheets are yours if you request one from a publishing house and include a self-addressed, stamped envelope. If you collect and study several fact sheets, you'll have a good idea of what the market will bear at the time you're writing.

Other ways to find out what's hot these days is to ask the manager of local bookstores. You should also devour newspaper and television ads for books. Read the *New York Times Book Review* every Sunday and invest in a subscription to *Publishers Weekly*, a trade magazine for writers and other professionals in the publishing field. The address is R.R. Bowker Co., 1180 Avenue of the Americas, New York NY 10036.

KNOW YOUR SUBJECT

The next step is to know as much as possible about your subject. Fiction is usually dull and unimpressive without facts to back it up and give it life. The best selling novels are often those which satisfy the reader's curiosity with rich details such as how a war was won or lost, how crime rings are broken, or how something actually works. Arthur Hailey's *Hotel* was enchanting because he included behind-the-scenes facts about hotels; for example, the way poor people are hired to sift through the muck and rescue silverware that is carelessly tossed down garbage chutes. Pulitzer Prize winner James A. Michener's books, such as *Hawaii* or *Centennial*, deeply probe the real history and social patterns of a geographic area. Norman Mailer, in writing his "true-life" novel, *The Executioner's Song*, plowed through reams of convict Gary Gilmore's letters and court documents, interviewing almost everyone who ever knew the man. Mailer needed research assistants to help him do the job. In his afterword to the novel, Mailer tells the reader what his research entailed:

> "This book does its best to be a factual account of the activities of Gary Gilmore and the men and women associated with him. In consequence, *The Executioner's Song* is directly based on interviews, documents, records of court proceedings, and other original material that came from a number of trips to Utah and Oregon. More than one hundred people were interviewed face to face, plus a good number talked to by telephone. The total, before count was lost, came to something like three hundred separate sessions . . . "

This stubborn research gave Mailer the facts he needed to build a heart-thumping account of Gilmore's brutal life and death. It's the little truths—lines of Gilmore's poetry, letters detailing his love and loyalty to his girl friend, and real people recounting the way he developed his vicious temper—that keep the reader going through Mailer's 1050-page novel. The book is more than entertainment. It's an education in psychology, sociology, criminal law, and prison life. Readers like to know they're learning something real while they turn the pages. And they depend on you, the author, to do the research that will help them.

PRIMARY AND SECONDARY SOURCES

There are two ways to do research: through primary sources, and secondary sources. Primary sources are ways to find information that nobody has yet written down. They are your own observations, experiences, and interviews with people upon whom you wish to base your characters. You should also talk to people who have had the experience about which you want to write.

Secondary sources are written. They can usually be found in the library. They are reference books, subject books, dissertations, and newspapers, magazines, and other periodicals.

Most writers use a combination of primary and secondary sources. I go to secondary sources first, so I can bone up on a subject before I start asking people questions. That means I spend time in the library before taking my tape recorder and venturing into the field.

LOVE YOUR LIBRARY

James Michener says he visits the library more than once a week. He makes a beeline for the card catalog, which will help you locate a book by author or title. If you go through the catalog by subject headings, you'll come across exciting books you never dreamed were there. Browse along the library shelves, too. New books will pop out at you like unexpected treasures. They'll give you information and ideas.

There are all sorts of subject indexes—Art Index, Business Periodicals Index, and the Social Sciences Index, to name a few—which will tell you where to find specific information. And there are endless biographical sources. These can start your mind clicking on a character.

One day while browsing through a 1969 edition of *Current Biography*, I found a tiny photo of blind singer and guitarist Jose Feliciano. Along with the photo was a heart-rending story about how the singer started his career. He begged restaurant owners to let him, "a simple poor blind kid," come in out of the cold and tune up his guitar. Of course, instead of tuning, he played for the guests.

What guts! What an inspiration for a fictional character!

In the *Dictionary of American Biography*, I found a four-page story on the life of Clara Barton, who started the American Red Cross. The biographer described Barton as a spoiled child who grew into a determined, strong-willed woman, "unable to act as a subordinate gracefully or to cooperate easily." She was even physically described as a petite, slender woman who marched—not walked—into a room, wth her head held high. These traits apparently made Barton an unusual woman for her times, and if I wanted to do a short story or novel on a spunky lady who lived during that period (1821-1912), I couldn't find a better source for initial inspiration and information than that dictionary.

RESEARCH IS FUN

Library research is just one source for fiction writers. Some writers use it only sparingly. They have more fun with on-the-spot research. So they rely on travel for detail and authenticity; on interviewing to catch the sounds and sights of people as they react to news or emotions; on personal experience; and on astute observation of everyday events.

This type of research can be expensive, because you invest time and money traveling to locations about which you want to write. But it pays off. There's usually no good substitute for *being* where your imaginary action takes place, or talking to real people who live there. It would be hard to believe that novelist Leon Uris wasn't in Cyprus when he described it in the first few pages of *Exodus*:

> "The flatness, the yellow stone houses with their red tiled roofs, the sea of date palms. The road ran alongside the ancient Venetian wall which was built in a perfect circle and surrounded the old city. Mark could see the twin minarets that spiraled over the skyline from the Turkish section of the old city. The minarets that belonged to St. Sophia's, that magnificent crusader cathedral turned into a Moslem mosque. As they drove along the wall they passed the enormous ramparts shaped like arrowheads."

Descriptions like this spice fiction with details that attract and hold reader interest, and draw readers into your story. And they show that the author knows something about what he's seeing: Uris researched the origin of the minarets, and informed the reader they belonged to a cathedral that was turned into a mosque.

Why go to all that trouble? Because research provides a strong footing for your fiction and makes readers identify with what you say. They feel part of the times, places, and people in your story.

Yes, fiction writers do make things up. They create characters and events. But fiction writers also need the anchor of reality, provided only by research.

Research provides a learning experience for you and your readers. It can be an exciting, fun-filled part of your writing. And, there's another reason why research is important: well-researched fiction is the kind that sells best.

* * *

Research does pay off, says author Frances Statham, who invests at least several months of reading, travel, and library research in each of her romance stories or Gothics. Gothics are novels usually characterized by the use of desolate, remote settings and mysterious incidents. They have complicated historical plots. Statham says she wouldn't dream of doing such a book without research to give her a full and accurate picture of the lifestyle and events of the times.

"To be a good writer, you can't be lazy about your research. A lot of people won't write about something that didn't happen to them, because they don't want to struggle with bits and pieces of information. But you have to do that, because publishers appreciate—and pay for—books that give the reader a little history lesson along with the plot.

"Even if you're not doing history, you must be correct about statements and events, or you'll lose credibility. I once read a novel by a British writer who had a female character in his book get into an auto accident. She had a head injury. This girl, the heroine, was taken to the hospital and given a sedative.

"I put the book down right there. As the former wife of a doctor, I know that you don't give sedatives to people with head injuries. That writer didn't do his research, and I lost faith in his writing."

Educate yourself during research. In his latest book, *Creation,* Gore Vidal traces the life of a fifth century Persian politician. To do it, he devoted six years to the study of history, religion, and philosophy.

Vidal said he chose a Persian hero because he thought the Persians were superior in many ways to the Greeks. And the Persians appealed to him because theirs was a more gentlemanly society and more settled, apparently, than Greece. "Also, I chose a Persian point of view from a desire to know more about the people, leaders, and culture of the times. I can only write about what interests me greatly . . . I've always been fascinated by Confucianism and Buddhism and as I taught myself, I put what I learned in the book."

Writers must love to learn, believes historian Elizabeth Stevenson. She writes biographies, such as the huge Macmillan book on Frederick Law Olmstead, *Park Maker*, and says fiction writers must be just as careful as she is about their facts.

"I'm a writer of nonfiction, but I know that fiction suffers greatly if it lacks authentic detail. It isn't hard to find those details. You know what I do when I research? I sit very quietly in the library, spying on the personal lives of others, getting stuff on people I'm going to write about. I concentrate on secondary sources, because since I'm doing history, all the people I'd talk to are dead.

"I start with a person's birth and slip in a three-by-five inch card for each important event in the person's life. Everything is done chronologically on little cards that I put neatly into files. I stack the files in an old bathtub in my home. Before

I'm ready to write, I may have six or seven boxes of files in the tub. But that means I'm never stumped for a fact, so I don't have to put off my writing, once I do get to it, to go and hunt down the answer to a research question."

Hunting for answers intrigues readers. If you've done careful research, your plot is likely to include enough fascinating facts to keep readers turning the pages. Perhaps few authors know that better than Martha Hennissart and Mary Jane Latsis, who write mystery novels together under the pseudonym Emma Lathen. These writers pick a complicated—and shady—business deal as their subject and build a murder mystery around it. In the process, they teach readers about banking, real estate, and other aspects of our industrial society. Books like *Banking on Death* earned the writers a review in the *Wall Street Journal* in March, 1981:

> "The authors say that most of their research for a new book involves living in a place awhile to get ideas for scenes and talking with people involved in an industry. (For their hockey book, they bought season tickets to the Boston Bruin games.) 'It's a form of impression-gathering rather than fact-finding,' Miss Hennissart says. 'We're gathering types for our characters, sort of an aura . . . Especially if you have the whiff of an academic researcher, it's amazing how much people will tell you.' "

Check on what people tell you, advises Pat Watters, a veteran magazine and book writer. He warns that interviews aren't always accurate because people love to make up things when they're talking to writers.

"My biggest project was a book on the Coca-Cola company, and it kept me in the library seven days a week, ten hours a day, for two months. Then I interviewed salespeople, executives, bottlers, and so on. All of it went down on tape. I also took a notepad, which I used to jot down descriptions of the person, what his office looks like, what gestures he makes—stuff you can't get on a tape recorder.

"I always ask for anecdotes. I was doing nonfiction, but what I got was enough for a lifetime of novels, too. I learned what the owners went through to keep Coke's formula a secret, and odd ways people tried to steal the secret.

"I discovered people love to tell you 'inside' stories, but you have to check on them. One guy told me he knew the original driver of the first Coke wagon. Sure, I wanted to interview the old fella! But when I told the public relations person at Coke how excited I was about it, he just cracked up. He said, 'Oh, that makes about one-hundred twenty-five men who drove that first wagon.' "

Readers tour story worlds through research. Terry Kay relied heavily on his knowledge of the rural American south to write *After Eli*. Kay feels that readers want to be led into times and places that are new and exciting for them. To do that, your research must be accurate.

"Why do people read? Mostly, for fun. They want to escape from their everyday lives. They want to be transported to places they might never visit in real life; they want to go back and forth in time. The writer is their tour guide. Nobody trusts a tour guide who isn't at home with the locale or who stumbles with the language. If you want to make the reader's trip enjoyable, you'd better bone up on where you're taking him."

Don't rush research, admonishes French-educated Rosemarie Simpson. If you devote enough time to researching your book, you'll produce a better product. You will know more about your subject and be more enthusiastic about it.

"It took me five years to complete the research for my novel, *The Seven Hills of Paradise*. Of course I was teaching at the time, as well as writing. Unless you're rich, you can't afford to drop everything and hide away in the library all the time. But every bit of time spent on that research was well worth it. My book is set in the thirteenth century, and it's not possible to learn about life in that period unless you really dig into it.

"Even more important, you must *feel* what life was like in the time period about which you wish to write. It took weeks of research before I could *feel* the slimy stone wall of a dungeon, and *feel* the cold drafts blowing through a castle.

"You must feel as if you're living every minute of the action that takes place in your novel. That feeling will come if you spend time researching."

Your emotion lives in characters.

Editor/writer Jack Lange dug into daily newspaper reports of 1913 to research his fictionalized account of the Leo Frank case, in which an innocent Jewish man was lynched for the murder of a little Southern girl.

"First, I read several books on the case. Then I went through the day-by-day reports in three different newspapers. By following the story so closely, I was able to get into the skins, into the heads, of the people involved. So I could *feel* their anguish and pain, *feel* what was going on in society at the time.

"When I wrote, this feeling made my characters more believable. They came alive almost by themselves. Words jumped from their mouths because I was inside them, feeling everything that was going on. Obviously, I was fabricating, but my research was what made the fabrication possible. I had learned so much about my subject that I was able to see the scenes, hear the words, smell the smells.

"I was living in 1913 through my research."

Personal observations serve as research. R.V. Cassill advises writers to pay close attention to sounds, smells, and body language. This helps writers tune in to the emotional environment of a place or person. He calls this type of research a "search for signals," in that it teaches writers to pick up on important details and discard those which are insignificant.

"Because you are looking specifically for material that will fit into and enhance your writing, you want to do some specific observing, some specific research. Some writers research first, then write. Others, who are more concerned with feeling their way through the plot and characters, might find the best technique is to start writing first, before you research, and let the research follow the needs of the character.

"For example, if the main character is going to go to Colorado to ski, that may be the time for the writer to go—not before. In nonfiction the research most often comes first, and is more organized. Fiction may not be planned. Its research may rely more on immediate need rather than long-range planning.

"But no matter how you do it, it's important to remember the search for signals, the tiny details of life, is a research tool that cannot be overlooked, no matter how well you think you know your subject."

Knowing your subject gives a head start, states multi-talented Dr. John Feegel. He is a physician, attorney, and novelist whose interests come together in writing mysteries with medical and legal elements in the plot. He started writing in 1972 "for my own enjoyment," publishing *Autopsy* in 1975. Since then he's also written about the CIA (Central Intelligence Agency), the Bay of Pigs, and trouble in a small Georgia town.

"My novel *The Dance Card* took about a year of research, since it concerned the Bay of Pigs affair, and I wanted to get precise information and dates into my book. For that, I went to the periodic literature of the times, such as newspapers and news magazines.

"*Malpractice* was done off the top of my head because it's about medicine; I had a big head start there because I'm a physician. My research was already part of my general fund of knowledge. I'd advise other writers who want to be accurate about precise fields, such as medicine, to consult with someone who is accustomed to the work and who can talk knowledgeably about it. Then, go back and check the texts to make sure the information is accurate and you aren't getting a slanted point of view.

"Better yet, stick to what you know. You may still have to do some research, but it won't consume you. Of course, there are some very fine writers who can go out, learn someone else's craft, and write about it. I'm thinking of Arthur Hailey [*Airport*, *Hotel*, *Wheels*] who can dive into the hotel or airline business and really devour all that information and detail. But most of us do best selecting a subject we know and care about, and supplementing our own knowledge with careful research."

Your interest in the research subject will grow, contends science fiction writer Michael Bishop. Once you learn about a subject, you can do several books, drawing on and enlarging your fund of knowledge as you go along.

"Anthropology fascinates me, so I've done several books that use the information I have on the subject. Every time I tackle a new story idea, I learn more about the same subject, so the research gets easier as I go along. It also gets deeper; you become almost an expert in the field. That's wonderful, because your interest will grow.

"My most recent novel, *No Enemy But Time*, amounts to an in-depth study of human evolution. A character goes back in time to learn about the first humans. Even though I already knew a lot about the subject, I found it necessary—and enjoyable—to spend a good deal more time on research. I read about twenty-five books on anthropology, and at least thirty magazine articles. I also toured a primate research center with a professional anthropologist.

"The book took three years of research and one year of writing. I got more and more interested. It won't be hard to write more books on the same subject. Knowledge doesn't dry up. It expands, and so does your mind. That's a good reason to do research. It's a joy."

5 | Creating Characters

FICTION IS CREATING stories about people and how they react to events around them. If you don't have people—or humanlike creatures—you don't have fiction. A good novel or short story explores the depths and heights of human emotion. It's much more than a dash from one adventure to the next. All the surprising twists of your plot are meaningless unless they happen to human beings.

The folks who are born, who sweat, love, and die in your short stories or novels are your characters. They carry out the action, talk about what they're doing and what's going on around them, cause and resolve conflicts, and eventually arrive at some new understanding of themselves that wasn't there when the book began.

Creation of believable characters is the fiction writer's most demanding task.

REAL PEOPLE

Some writers base their characters on real people. Adventure novelist Bill Diehl, for example, endows his fictional friends with the hair color, physical build, and even the names of people he knows. Diehl says these people get such a kick out of reading about the exploits of his fictionalized "offspring" that they come up to him at cocktail parties and beg, "Name your next hero after me, Bill," or "Can I get to be your next cop character?"

James Joyce's *Ulysses*, called one of the twentieth century's great experimental works of fiction, contained several actual people who were also called by their real names. Jacqueline Susann, author of *Valley of the Dolls*, was widely suspected of basing her pill-popping, rich-girl characters on famous people such as Judy Garland or Ethel Merman. Susann denied these charges on her frequent television appearances, but the denials only fueled reader interest and sold more copies of her book. Other widely read novels such as Marcel Proust's *Remembrance of Things Past* and Thomas Mann's *Magic Mountain* were also filled with characters copied from real life.

Other writers prefer to create characters from bits and pieces of people they know, like sewing a quilt from scraps. Terry Kay does this; he tucks a memory of someone's conversational style in his head, blends it with another person's physical appearance, and perhaps adds somebody else's childhood experiences. It all comes together as a character Kay thinks would act and react like a real person.

"GIVE A GUY A REASON..."

If your characters are to capture the attention, imagination, and loyalty of readers, they must live their fictional lives in a way that readers can understand. Your characters must be believable. "Give a guy a *reason* for doing something," says Diehl. "Don't just have a guy be a bastard for no good reason.

Maybe his dad beat him when he was a kid, and that's why he grew up to be bad. Maybe she got raped, and that's why she's frigid. You don't have to be a psychiatrist, but you do have to give your characters a past—maybe only a paragraph or two—that makes their present seem plausible."

Believable characters do believable things. The characters in your books or short stories have to contend with human frustrations, limitations, and problems. That doesn't mean pages of dull prose on your housewife's daily battle with toilet bowl cleanser. But suppose the thankless drudgery of endless housecleaning sets the stage for a bitter fight with her insensitive husband. He screams she's good for nothing else but cleaning toilets, and this reaffirms her self-loathing. The next day it all erupts in a murderous attack on her adorable toddler, who soils the toilet and innocently reminds Mom to clean it up.

Most people would recoil at a mother attacking her child. But they can understand it . . . if your writing ability builds up their familiarity with the character's frustrations and gives them sound psychological reasons as to *why* she reacted that way. You can effectively shock the reader with infanticide or other blood-boiling actions of your character if you surround the shock with past and present events that make up real problems. No matter what happens, you want your reader to sympathize with the character. Once sympathy is lost, your reader is probably lost, too. He puts down the book, and that's the end of your relationship.

LONG DISTANCE FRIENDSHIP

Readers and writers may never meet face to face, but they do have an intimate relationship. It's a long-distance friendship carried on through the speech and actions of the characters created by the writer and related to by the reader. Author Robert Stone, for example, reaches out to his readers with deep ideas discussed by his characters. The people in Stone's books do a lot of talking to one another—speech full of intellectual curiosity and emotional fireworks. This is Stone's way of conversing with readers. Other writers try to get even closer to readers by offering themselves as the major characters in their books. Some writers tell me that one of the first questions people ask them is, "Are you the main character?" Few writers would deny that some part of themselves comes out in one or more of their characters.

An enormous amount of planning and self-exploration goes into creating characters, whether they are based on the author, the author's friends and acquaintances, historical figures, or bits and pieces of all of these. Your character has to have certain looks (down to the last bump on his nose), an age, a place to live, a style of housekeeping, and a way of talking, walking, and wearing clothes. Then he needs a family to love and hate, friends and enemies, and perhaps a boss, an employee or a partner. He needs a past, and he's probably working toward—or avoiding—a future. How do writers come up with all of this? They absorb and borrow a lot of it from reality.

INTERVIEWING FOR FICTION

Many writers take notes when they meet interesting people, jotting down physical characteristics or odd mannerisms they think will wear well on a future fictional friend. Others use tape recorders. Anne Rivers Siddons tapes people's voices to study and remember how old-time Southerners speak. Later, the words and inflections she hears from real people tumble from the mouths of her characters. Paul Hemphill, who wrote *Long Gone,* says he spent time chatting with an old baseball pro so that he could obtain information and ideas that would later help shape the main characters in his novel.

"There were no real people like the people in my book," say Hemphill, "but after I talked to folks and lived some of the events myself, I knew that somewhere out there, there just *had*

73 Creating Characters

to be characters like the ones I was creating."

Writers say that creating characters is like giving birth: it's long and painful, but so rewarding that you want to go back and do it again and again. Many novelists say they feel like God when they make up a fictional person. After all, they are creating life.

The writer's challenge is to come up with make-believe people who have all the beauty and flaws of real people, who can make readers feel joy and sorrow. To dull some of the pain of such creation, fiction writers often employ some of the same interviewing techniques as journalists.

LOOK AND LISTEN

Quite a few successful fictionalists were once newspaper or magazine writers. One of the things they learned by writing nonfiction is how to look at and listen to real people. Later, they would modify and reconstruct the features of these people to fit fictional characters. Ernest Hemingway was a journalist first, and a fiction writer later.

Journalists use interviews to learn about people and the events that shape their lives. Fiction writers, too, must "interview" in one way or another by careful listening and observing, intimate interaction, or actually sitting down with people and recording their answers to predetermined questions.

To some extent this interviewing is an invasion of privacy. It tests the writer's ability and willingness to overcome his own insecurity about probing into people's lives. But it is necessary. Author and teacher John Brady says in his book, *The Craft of Interviewing*, that this is hard for writers because most of them are "private people." But, he adds, when you inteview it is "a matter of professional—and, one hopes, genuine—curiosity overtaking the writer's innate shyness."

* * *

Shyness hinders writers, says Terry Kay. It keeps them from exploring themselves and others, and thus delving deep enough to develop real character. Kay is a former theater critic whose novel, *After Eli*, is being made into a movie.

"It wouldn't do at all for me to be shy about collecting information about my writing, because so much of what goes into my stories comes from real people. I coax them into telling stories I can later embellish.

"I collect Southern stories, and the best way to do that is to engage people in conversation. I guide them into a topic, then sit and listen. I might ask a bunch of old farmers at the country store, 'Ever hear of any ghost stories around here?' They'll go on and on.

"Most of the traits found in my fictional characters come from real people. They are people I interview because something about them interests me. Later, a fragment of that real person's character will fill out my fictional person.

"My main character in *After Eli* is named Michael. He is a composite of some real people mixed with fictional people I read about or watched in movies or on TV. And some characteristics of Michael's are also mine: patience, an Irish backgound, the love of being theatrical. To get those qualities out, I interviewed myself. I do it often; I talk out loud to myself. I do it when I'm alone, but once in a while I can even do it in front of others.

"If I've been writing a long time and I feel the need to get out and be with other people, I'll sometimes go into a bar and pretend I'm the character I'm writing about. I lie like crazy. I adopt the mannerisms and way of talking of my character, and see how people react to him. It makes me really get into the skin of that character. I can hear the dialogue coming from myself; I can hear the real conversation going on around me.

"I couldn't do that if I was shy. If I was shy, I'd probably never ask any questions, never get any answers. Then I wouldn't be able to write."

Dare to ask questions, challenges Bill Cutler, a former professor of English at Columbia University. He specializes in interviewing, using the techniques of fiction to draw word pictures of real characters and make readers relate to them.

"I do a lot of restaurant reviews. You might not think there's room for creative writing here, but there is. Suppose I go into a soul food restaurant. Part of my job is to get the facts, but there is a lot of opinion mixed in, too. I want to get the feel of the place. I'm looking for more than food prices. I want to capture atmosphere, to figure out what makes this restaurant and its people tick.

"First, I eat. I have to *do* the thing I'm writing about. That's a rule, I think, that applies to fiction and nonfiction. If I'm writing about restaurant people, I must eat their food. I can't pretend I know what it's all about until I do it. If I pretend, I'll never learn anything.

"Soon I start a conversation with the person I want to interview. It's casual and quiet. While we chat I take good mental notes about how that person looks and acts, and the way he or she relates to me and to the questions I ask about the thing under discussion—in this case, the restaurant and the food. The notes soon go down on paper. I start writing things down as soon as I sense the person is at ease with me and with the idea of being interviewed.

"I gave the example of a soul food restaurant. Let's assume I never ate that kind of food before. In fact, I'm not sure I know what soul food really *is*. This is where the daring to ask questions comes in. It takes some experience. A beginner might not ask that restaurant owner, 'Say, what *is* soul food? Could you name some soul foods for me, and explain what they are? Can you tell me how they got the name of soul food, and what that means to you?' The beginner is afraid to ask, because he thinks the owner will decide he's stupid.

"This fear is in all writers, fiction as well as nonfiction.

They are afraid to ask what goes on inside, whether it's inside a restaurant or inside a person. But you have to admit you don't understand. Ask the damned question. And ask it again and again until you *do* understand. Sometimes you will make mistakes, ask foolish questions, be turned away. So what? You can learn from that, too."

Learn from nonfiction, suggests newspaperman and fiction writer Chet Fuller. His latest book, *I Hear Them Calling My Name,* won numerous journalistic awards. Some of the people he interviewed for that nonfiction book will later appear as fictional characters in a novel.

"I learned a lot about writing fiction from my nonfiction training. I rely on journalism, especially journalistic interviewing, to supply me with fictional characters.

"When I was doing some newspaper stories I met a real 108-year-old man who gave me firsthand accounts of the Civil War. Later, I used him as a fictional character. I made him into an old woman in my novel. This old woman keeps a shotgun. She calls it Matthew. She gave her gun a name! I'd never come up with an idea like that on my own. I got it from the old man I interviewed. He really did have a gun with a name.

"I'd say about fifty percent of my fictional characters owe their births to a real person I've interviewed. I listen very carefully for dialect. I pay attention to pauses, silences, the things people *don't* say. In fiction you can't put down everything a person says. It would be boring. You must edit to get straight to the meat of the conversation. Along the way you describe facial expressions, body language, the things that substitute for speech. They say a lot.

"Listening to real people is very important for fiction writers. Journalistic training helps you learn to do this. If you know how to listen for and capture speech, it makes the characters in your fiction ring true. You have to listen for the differences in people's speech patterns, the cultural differences between races, generations, sexes. My father's generation, for example, has a different concept of time than my generation, and it shows up in his speech. Ask my father when he's coming home from the store, and he'll say, 'Directly.' Ask me when I'm coming home, and I'll look at my watch and say, 'In thirty minutes.'

"Those are real differences. If you neglect them in your fiction, it won't have the ring of truth."

Truth puts flesh on fictional characters, says editor and playwright Jack Lange. He says some characters in his play about the 1913 Leo Frank case are based on real people; others are created characters designed to add drama or simplify the plot.

"Some of the characters are pretty true to life, like Leo Frank, the main person in the story. He was a real man. He was really accused of killing a little girl. He was really dragged out and hanged, and he was probably really framed.

"I got as close to Leo Frank as I could by reading books and newspaper stories about him. But obviously I'm fabricating because I put words in his mouth I couldn't possibly know were there. They were words he would likely use, not words he *did* use.

"I did something else a lot of fiction writers do: I created composite characters. For example, there were a lot of reporters on that case, but I narrowed it down to just two. I made them up; I made suppositions about what they were thinking and who they were. It cut down on a lot of confusion in the plot.

"In doing all this, I tried to create the kinds of personalities I think were at least capable of behaving in the way I said they did, and likely to say the words I put in their mouths. My purpose was to get inside their skins, inside their heads. I put myself in their shoes. At the same time I was writing about a real historical event, so I had to be as true as possible to the written record.

"You enter a different level of reality when you're writing fiction, or trying to zoom back and forth beween a real historical event and your fictional interpretation of that event. Your characters were once real if you are writing about history, and now you must make them live again. Only now they live at *your* command."

"Look inside" for characters and draw them from your own imagination. That's the advice of editor Larry Ashmead of Harper & Row. He prefers reading about characters who were born entirely in the writer's mind.

"I see very little percentage for a novelist in using real people as models for their fictional characters. It's a limited technique. Once you decide to base a character in a novel on a real person, you're limiting your imagination and creativity. Using real historical characters is an interesting gimmick, but mainly it's the novelist's job to create, not borrow. Most novelists with whom I work create characters out of whole cloth, and that's the usual successful technique as far as I'm concerned."

It's safer to create characters, says attorney Louis Isaf. He handles contracts and legal problems for writers, suggesting that the best way to stay out of trouble is to avoid using real people in your fiction.

"If you can stay away from borrowing real people for your stories and novels, then stay away. Some writers think they'll play it safe and get the person's consent. But in a novel you never really know, in the long run, what you'll wind up having that character say or do. So getting consent may not work.

79 Creating Characters

What is the person consenting to?

"Of course, most of the time you have no trouble at all. If somebody does get mad enough to resort to legal action, there are various degrees of defense. Is the person a public figure? If so, you can probably use him or her. For libel or slander cases, your defense is truth. But remember the charge of invasion of privacy, and be aware that someone who is not a public figure has a right to remain out of view—and out of your book.

"If you feel strongly that you must use a certain real person in your fiction it's best to disguise the character so the person can't easily identify himself. If all you're going to do is use the name, and nothing else is similar, you can probably get away with it. If the name is very unique—Isaf, for example—you'd better get written permission."

Use only bits and pieces of real people and you won't *need* permission, says science fiction author Damon Knight. The characters in Knight's many novels and short stories are mostly composites of people, liberally fleshed out by the author's imagination.

"Most of the time I base my characters on bits and pieces of real people: a voice from one, a smile from another, perhaps a limp from someone else. You can't make up a whole person without resorting to these bits and pieces, because if you do it will probably turn out to be a cliché; you will no doubt wind up basing your character on other fictional characters. Remember, you don't use *all* of a real person's characteristics. You don't want to copy a real person exactly. You want a character who explains himself easily, and whose actions are quickly understandable to the reader. So he needs a past, as well as a present and a future. The past is what makes him act this way. The present is the conflict in the story. The future is the big unknown, the surprise for the reader."

Characters should surprise readers, says Frances Statham. She plans each of her romantic sagas so that her heroine confronts a problem and makes the reader gasp at the way she solves it.

"Your character is in the book to point the way to your major theme. To develop character, make the reader pull for your man or woman. Give the main character a problem to solve. Once you get rolling in solving it, if you set things up right, your main person will grow.

"When I start a novel I know exactly what each character looks like. And each one has to change—get better or worse—during their course of baptism by fire in the book. I like to give each character an eccentricity to make them more human. My heroine in *Flame of New Orleans* is deathly afraid of water. So what happens to her? She is forced to make a dangerous crossing over water. She must conquer her inner fear. That provides drama for the story and makes the character grow. She does something she's afraid of, and thus moves on."

Experience your character's emotions, suggests novelist Mary Lee Settle. She won the National Book Award in 1978 for *Blood Tie*, and is now finishing a five-book historical saga. She told *The New York Times Book Review* in October, 1980, that part of her research involves putting herself in her character's shoes.

"You have to give yourself a kind of organized memory. You have to get a concept of being in the past, almost self-hypnosis. I was concerned not so much with what happened—that's easy, it's in the history books—as I was with what people at the time *thought* was happening. I had to experience their awareness and their blindness . . . It's not right to give a writer too much protection. We're not eggs. Writers are part actors. [You can] imagine being a murderer from the experience of swatting a fly."

81 Creating Characters

Characters shouldn't do the impossible, says Stuart Woods. Keep your characters struggling with real problems, and have have them suffer until they come up with sensible solutions. Nobody believes a character who comes out of every scrape unscathed.

"Above all, you want your characters to be believable. You make a character live by showing him in all his humanness, all his silliness, all his inability to solve problems at the snap of a finger.

"I put my characters together out of bits and pieces of other characters and some real people. In the end I come up with an individual who is believable. Basing your character on a real person is no guarantee that he or she will have that quality of believability. Even real people can ring false. Instinct on your part will tell you if your character, or something your character is doing, is believable. One of my main characters in *Chiefs* gets killed by accident. That's very real.

"I also like to have real figures—like the great president FDR—in my books. They make brief appearances, and they always do believable, human things. In *Chiefs* the future president of the nation shows a weakness for chocolate sodas. *The Winds of War* and *Ragtime* were books which also successfully employed real historical figures.

"But real or made up, historical or not, be sure your characters don't perform impossible feats or get into situations nobody could resolve. Don't do it even if you've read in the newspapers that somebody really did it, or you know about it yourself. It won't be good if the reader doesn't believe it. My editor says, 'The fact that it's true is no excuse.' "

6 | Plots and Plans

ORGANIZING A WORK of fiction is one of the writer's most serious and difficult tasks. When you are seized by the joyful and urgent desire to write, it's hard to temporarily dam the gush of words until you've carved out the proper channels through which the tide must flow. But unless you discipline talent with organization, the result is a flood of thought that only confuses and irritates readers. Good fiction takes planning.

Planning also makes it easier to get words on paper; you'll be more creative if you don't have to stop every few sentences to grumble, "What comes next?" You'll already know, because your plot—call it a blueprint, map, outline, plan, or guide—will tell you.

CHARACTERS "MISBEHAVE"

Good writers are well-organized. Many of them nurse both their first and last sentences in their heads for some time before they write them down. In the meantime, they outline the great middle portion of their novels or short stories. The outline can be a general ten-page wrapup of what the characters do, the problems they confront, and how things all work out at the end. Or it can span fifty pages or more, and include charts of action, lists of characters' traits, and detailed descriptions of environment. Usually, the more detailed the better. Unless you're a very experienced writer, you're bound to start sweating when things don't turn out as you pictured them in your mind. Ficticious characters and events have a way of twisting themselves out of your grasp, like children who misbehave. Seasoned writers can accept that misbehavior with good humor, and even welcome it as Truman Capote does when he calls such misbehavior "the unexpected dividend." Capote says his novels are usually completely organized in his mind before he puts down a single word, but surprises do come along.

"I invariably have the illusion that the whole play of a story, its start, middle and finish, occurs in my mind simultaneously—that I'm seeing it in one flash. But in the working-out, the writing-out, infinite surprises happen. Thank God, because the surprise, the twist, the phrase that comes at the right moment out of nowhere, is the unexpected dividend, that joyful little push that keeps a writer going."

But you can't count on surprises to produce a well-rounded story. For that, you need organization. And organization means the careful, conscious construction of a plot. It means creating biographies for your major characters, boiling your theme down to a few succinct words, fixing your story's ambience firmly in your mind, and writing down key descriptions of place and atmosphere. Careful writers also know, well in advance, how their characters will resolve the major conflicts in the story. Very little is left to chance.

ARE OUTLINES CONTRIVED?

Some writers scoff at outlining, believing it's too contrived. Fletcher Knebel, author of *Vanished, Seven Days in May,* and *Crossing in Berlin,* says he often has no idea where a book is going, and likes the sudden self-surprise that comes when the story switches. "I don't know how those guys write who have everything charted out like an engineer's blueprint," he says. "What's the fun of that? It's like filling in a crossword puzzle."

Other writers claim fiction *is* a puzzle, to be pieced together bit by bit until the whole picture emerges. John Irving, author of *The World According to Garp,* says his book took four years to write, and that most of it was like pasting together "the pieces of a filmcutter's work." Historian and author Charles L. Mee, Jr., looks upon writing "as a painter works on a painting . . . You can come to the work as if it's on a canvas, start at the upper corner, or sketch some other subjects in, or rework it ten or fifteen times." Thomas Wolfe once told his agent that his novels were done in bits and pieces and resembled "the bones of some great prehistoric animal." But Wolfe was careful to assemble those bones in final form before he let an editor see his work. He organized chunks of scenes, crafted elaborate outlines, and polished and revised many times.

SUBCONSCIOUS PLANNING

I suspect that authors who sneer at written outlines have a powerful subconscious. They're probably plotting and planning without even knowing it. Then, when it's time to write, the words just seem to pour out. But those words are really the end result of a deep-seated inner process of selection. If they're fussy about what they select, these subconscious planners will have less rewriting to do when they finally put things down on paper.

Careful organization and intricate written outlines usually

do cut down on the task of rewriting. Some writers who say they don't outline are merely planning at the end of the first writing period, rather than at the beginning. They apparently prefer to spill the story in one or several creative bursts, then go back and rewrite until it flows smoothly. Most writers eventually wind up working both ways: planning at the start, and rewriting when the first draft is on paper. Planning provides a path to follow. Rewriting sharpens both plot and prose, and helps eliminate obvious faults in the story, such as a weak ending. You might not spot those misconstructions the first time around.

THINK BEFORE YOU WRITE

There might be more disagreement about how to plan and organize fiction than about any other aspect of writing. Methods vary greatly, and writers change those methods as they mature. There is no set way to think before the words go down on paper; there's just a vague, general agreement among professional writers that it must be done. A novelist who starts with carefully planned written plots may eventually decide he's better at subconscious organization. Or, a "head planner" might tire of so much cranial exercise in advance of each book and take to writing out the plot and characterization of every scene.

Beginners usually do best if they think out and write down the skeleton of stories before they put flesh on fiction. Eventually, each writer comes up with a method of outlining and organizing that best fits his own particular needs. The methods can be borrowed from other writers or invented after personal trial and error. The most important task is to develop the discipline it takes to devise *some* method of thinking before you write.

* * *

Outline characters first, says Tom Cook. Cook, who writes both literary and popular novels, says the difference between them is that literary novels embrace ideas, while popular novels run on what happens next. To do either, he says, a writer must start with a thorough outline of his main character.

"In most cases, any type of novel relies on good characterization. So I really concentrate on knowing my characters very well. While I don't normally need a written outline, the characters and settings in my fiction are very firmly set down in my mind before I start the first sentence. I know the ending of the book about halfway through. If it's what I call a literary novel, the idea goes far beyond the character. The character either embodies the idea or creates the atmosphere in which the idea develops. All this takes a lot of pre-thought. Sometimes plot changes slightly; sometimes I have to change what happens if I think the events I've planned will force my characters to do something unnatural. If I have a good mental road map, however, changes remain slight. My characters all do what I'd intended. They understand each other and are capable of drawing out the idea that each embodies."

Planning starts early, stresses Stuart Woods, who planned his second book while he was finishing his first. As he wrote the first book, Woods was on the lookout for characters or subplots he could use in the construction of a new novel.

"One reason I could even think about a second book is that my first was pretty tightly organized. To even begin, I had to hand my publisher an outline and 200 completed pages which followed that outline. I didn't always know the exact words I was going to use, but I did have quite specific ideas about what would happen in each chapter. I also wanted to let the publisher see I knew how my book would begin and end.

"My first novel is complex. A lot of things happen to a lot

of different people. In one scene, a policeman is called in to stop a quarrel between a man and his wife. The man is beating his wife, and there's a new baby in the house. Later, I realized that a main character in my book number two would be that new baby.

"There it was: my first step in planning a new book. I immediately started outlining a scene in the second book which tied in with the situation in the first book. I wanted the beating to be a key factor in shaping the baby's personality—the personality of my new character. So you can see that I really do plan ahead, and very early. I've already written the last sentence of my next book. It's been in my head for years."

Pre-plan in your head, advises novelist Robert Newton Peck. He is the author of *A Day No Pigs Would Die*, *Fawn*, and *Kirk's Lane*, among others, and usually turns out three or four books a year.

"I never do an outline on paper. It's all skull work beforehand. Besides, fiction is based on characters, and on what characters do. They sometimes do things you can't plan out. In fiction you have strong people who want to act. They act out of greed, mostly. It's the character, not your pre-digested plot, who determines the book.

"If your character is weak, that will sometimes give you a different ending. Often I don't know how things are going to end until I'm on the last chapter.

"The things you do think out in advance are your time frame—is it taking place in 1920, say, or 1982?—your locale, and the issues at stake. This last thing is your plot. Plot is two dogs and a bone: the bone is at stake. That's the dramatic situation. Once I've thought out my dramatic situation, I'm ready to start writing.

"Fiction needs a conflict. Somebody wants something, tries to get it, and is opposed by somebody else. If Fido has a bone and Rover wants it but Fido won't give it to him, you've got a story if Rover really goes after that bone with all he's got. You need two contestants and a prize. You need two armies and one fort, two men and one woman, two grabby corporate vice presidents and one presidential vacancy. Who will win the tussle?

"Fiction is musical chairs. The most important thing for you to plan is how to set up nineteen chairs and twenty asses. Because if there are twenty chairs, nobody hustles."

Characters move; the plot follows, according to *Sharky's Machine* author Bill Diehl. He claims that if his characters are meticulously outlined in advance, it's easier to plan out the novel's plot.

"On the wall of my office is a huge white bulletin board. On that board I have headings like 'Prologue,' 'Book I,' 'Book II,' 'Subplots,' and 'Characters.' Tacked on to the head of 'Characters' is a thick sheaf of papers with each character's name, and brief paragraphs of description. I also put down who they are and what functions they perform in the book.

"First I create the character. Then I go back and fill in a biography for that character. I know how he grew up, what motivates him, if his father was an alcoholic, all the background stuff. I think readers like to know about a character's childhood and early experiences.

"I don't outline plots. I can wrap things up if my characters all stay in line. In the end it will all come together as long as I've outlined the characters in advance.

"I know what characters to use to provide drama, and which ones will provide comic relief. In *Sharky's Machine*, for example, I needed a lovable guy to help break the tension. Somebody funny. So I used my friend Larry to create a character called The Nosh. Larry, like The Nosh, knows how to do bugging and electronic stuff. I used him pretty straight, but I didn't tell him what I was going to do. I told his wife. I also told her what I didn't tell Larry: that The Nosh gets killed. So when Larry finally read the book and realized that The Nosh was him, he called me at three in the morning and he was crying! He was crying because he just came to the part where he dies! I wouldn't pick just anybody to model my characters after. I pick wonderful people: my friends. Otherwise if I picked a jerk, he might get mad and sue me.

"Oh, one more reason why I outline characters, but not plots: I want to know my characters very well, and really don't want them pulling tricks on me. But sometimes I do think of tricks, silly things to stick in the plot. I might have a crazy idea, like a bear drinking a beer in a bar, or a team of midgets playing basketball. If the idea amuses me, I put it in one of my chapters. I find a place where it will fit, and make the plot curve around and embrace the idea. I couldn't do that if everything was rigidly outlined up front."

Outlines impress publishers, according to long-time novelist Dean R. Koontz. Koontz, the author of fifty novels, has written comedy, suspense, and science fiction.

"I write from outlines. Most of the time the outline has already been sold to a publisher. He or she wants to read a clear picture of what you have in mind. It's rare that someone sells a book idea without an outline to back it up. Your careful outline is like a pact with the publisher, a way of telling him or her that you are serious about what you're doing, and capable of carrying it through.

"My outlines are done scene by scene or chapter by chapter. First, I choose the major scenes. Then, I set them up like flagstones in a wet garden; I'm concerned with how the reader will make his way through that garden. Later I can fill in the flowers (the details) between scenes.

Plots and Plans

"I never start a book unless I know the fate of the characters: who will die, who will marry whom. The characters remain true, even if the plot wanders. If I have a large outline I may not even use it, except the end. I *always* keep the end intact. Knowing the ending of the book reinforces the point I'm trying to make. No matter what happens, the structure is steady if I know the end.

"You might hand your publisher a thirty-page outline. From that, he'll expect a manuscript of about four hundred fifty pages. Sometimes in my case only seven or eight of the original outline pages come out of the book. And about three quarters of that concerns the end.

"I also find that research is a tremendous help in organizing and outlining the book. If you get the bits and pieces of research organized before you start writing, if the background is accurate and the events chronologically correct, it will carry you right along.

Experience comes later, observes seventy-nine-year-old mystery writer Lawrence Treat. The author of three hundred short stories and twenty novels, Treat started his career during the Depression, selling "mystery puzzles," which were brief tales of imagined crimes. Treat supplied clues to help readers solve the mystery. It was hard to sell books in the money-tight 1930s, but Treat's puzzles did well and he went on to novels.

At first, he says, he used to draw up charts for his books. "That was when I didn't have too much confidence. I had vertical columns for the chapters and then across I had squares to write in what was going on with plot, character, clues. I don't consciously do plotting any longer. I work mostly from character . . . if you do have a gimmick that's something you have to work up to."

Work up to complicated plots, suggests Lawrence Block. His monthly columns of advice on fiction have recently been gathered into a new book, *Telling Lies for Fun and Profit*. The term that Block uses for working up to plot events is "foreshadowing."

"Through skillful foreshadowing the writer prepares the reader for a sharp turn in the plot without tipping his hand altogether. The reader knows the turn is coming but doesn't know what sort of beast is lurking around the bend . . . Toward the end of *The Dead Zone*, Stephen King's novel that pits a clairvoyant against a potential despot, the plot is literally advanced by a bolt out of the blue. Johnny Smith, the prescient hero, is given the foreknowledge that a roadhouse where a graduation party is to be held will be struck by lightning. He tries to get the party canceled . . . Lightning strikes, as we know it will . . . How admirable of Stephen King to have laid the groundwork so carefully. How meticulously he must have plotted his book in advance in order to set up that business with the lightning rods (which figure greatly in the disaster) . . ."

Be firm but flexible, advises Damon Knight. Knight believes in clear outlining and tight organization, but remains flexible enough to anticipate—and even welcome—changes in parts of the plot.

"I do outline, but the outline modifies itself as I go along. For a short story, I outline five or six scenes. For a novel, I try to have a very clear idea of structure, which is where I'm going and how I'll get there. It's also important to know the beginning and ending. The material in between does change as I write.

"I advise other writers to be flexible and leave room in your outline for such changes. Do have a clear idea of place; know the area where your action is happening. That way your descriptions will come alive and you won't have to strain for the sounds and smells and textures of the environment around the characters. And, even if parts of the plot stray from your outline, other vital elements will remain constant. It will eliminate confusion if and when changes do occur to you."

Outlining spurs creativity, Anne Rivers Siddons

believes. The writing in her novels conjures up a constant parade of sparkling images; she says that outling a book frees her to concentrate on the creativity of words.

"I make simple charts, putting down when my characters were born, married and died. I always put in the year. The plot comes with the outline, which is a fifteen- or twenty-page synopsis of the novel. When I have those things down, I can write more freely and feel that my energies are more creatively spent.

"Things do change as I go along. But the characters usually mature as I had orginally intended. I knew Maggie, one of my characters in *Heartbreak Hotel*, like the back of my hand.

"It's hard on a writer when things change so much that you have to revamp your outline and do a lot of revising. That happened to me when I wrote *Fox's Earth*. It took me three years to write. Then it was rewritten and cut over a five-month period. I got it down to 965 pages, then redid a pivotal character. When the character was redone, a change had to be made in every page thereafter. And when I realized that, I sat down in the middle of my room and cried for three hours! I couldn't stand the idea of all that extra work. But it was like being three quarters of the way through labor. It hurts a lot, but you can't stop."

Organization keeps characters in line, declares

Robert Stone. His novels include *A Hall of Mirrors*, which won the Faulkner Award for best first novel in 1968, and *Dog Soldiers*, which in 1974 won the National Book Award for fiction. Stone's new novel, *A Flag for Sunrise*, focuses on angry Americans participating in Central America's revolutions. Stone keeps a firm hold on his characters by sticking to an outline.

"I didn't develop early as a writer. It took me a long time to learn the trade—organization and all that—and I write very, very slowly now. My most important thing in constructing a novel is to outline my characters. I want my characters to speak for themselves. They all have a voice, a way of talking, a theme, and a way of looking at the world. As you go on, characters may surprise you. Sometimes, out of their own strength, they change the plot. But you have to stay in control, and you do it with much organization. If your characters run away with things, you lose your sense of organization. If that happens, it's probably time to take a break of about a month from writing."

Questions help organize a novel, says Sol Stein, author and president of Stein & Day publishing. Stein has written *The Magician*, among other novels, and subjects other authors to intensive questioning before he will accept their book proposals. He says those questions help novelists find the really important elements of their work and organize around those elements.

"On any Monday morning, some writer will have a proposal for me. It will say 'I want to write a story about a janitor who is going to explode a plastic bomb in the men's urinal in the Department of Defense . . .'

"Then I ask, 'Who is the janitor? Is he a Polish resistance fighter? Where does he live?' And the more I ask, the further away we get from the plot.

"We hone in on *character*. That's where the story is: in the character. Yet most proposals center on plot. That's the big mistake.

Plots and Plans

"Your book has to create an emotional effect on the audience. Your leading character has to want something very badly. The more important that thing is, and the more your character wants it, the better your novel will be. Unless you have this conflict—this drama—you'd don't have a novel.

"You can find the essential elements in your novel by asking yourself questions about character and drama. Don't wait for the editor to do it; it may never happen. When the answers to the questions come clear, you'll be in a better position to organize plot around character. Questions of an exploring nature should be part of any writer's planning process."

7 | Begin and End with a Bang

I HAD STRANGE DREAMS in New York's IND subway. At 10 p.m., when it was cold and black in the city, I'd huddle on a plastic seat, dozing on my way home to Long Island from New York University's school of journalism.

My head was filled with words. Suddenly, in my dream, the top of my skull flipped open like a hinged box and the words poured out. They swirled around me like sea gulls, then melted in the smutty subway air. Then my head-flap banged shut and I could rest, swaying gently with the rumble of the train.

Somewhere in the stream of words, I always found the first line of an article or story I wanted to write. Sometimes a whole first paragraph came out. For years, that's how I began my writing.

I don't ride the subway anymore. My first lines and paragraphs come to me now while I'm jogging, or rinsing the dinner salad. Once they're down on paper I can go on with the rest of my story. If I don't have a good beginning, I'm stuck.

START RIGHT, OR REWRITE

Many writers say the same thing: full outlines for any type of writing elude them until they've thought out the critical opening lines. But some professionals tell me they force themselves to write even if they're not satisfied with the beginning *or* end of their stories. They rewrite, rather than rely on immediate inspiration.

Lawrence Block, for example, says the first lines and paragraphs of his beginning chapters almost always need rewriting. But he has to do that rewriting *before* he starts on chapter two. Otherwise, the imperfect opening lines bother him while he's writing the rest of the book.

FIND A TECHNIQUE

There is no set way to begin or end. In his book, *Writing the Novel from Plot to Print*, Block says every writer eventually finds his own technique.

"There are two schools of thought about the opening of a novel," he says. "One holds that the important thing is to get it written, the other that the important thing is to get it right. Both of them are quite valid, of course; the distinction is one of emphasis, and it will vary with the writer and with the particular novel."

Block usually starts his novels in the middle of the action. Maybe somebody is dragging a corpse down a deserted street. He lets the action go on breathlessly for a chapter or two. After the reader is hooked with action, Block goes back and tells him what is going on. He uses flashbacks to explain what he calls "the opening gambit."

R.V. Cassill likes to open with sentences that immediately thrust important information at the reader. "In the beginning, there is an utterance. Then there is explanation." The opening sentence puts the reader in the place where the story will unfold (the setting) and into the proper mood.

Cassill admits stories that open with action are usually better than stories that open with description or a character's words. Action *is* more exciting. But it also plunges the reader into the plot so fast that he doesn't have time to think about your theme. So, if theme is important to you, start slowly.

Whether you shove the reader into the story with action or guide him with description is mostly a matter of personal preference. A lot will depend on the tone of your book. Is it a thriller? These do best with action-packed opening scenes. Is it a novel or short story of theme and symbolism? Then perhaps poetic description is best for openers. Read openings you like, analyze them, and model your beginnings on the work of others whose writing pleases you.

JOURNALISTIC LEADS

In journalism, the beginning is called a *lead*, of which there are several types. The *query lead* opens with an abrupt question. It can be posed by the writer, or, if it's in quotes, by the person being interviewed. The *summary lead* wraps up critical information in the story, usually for people who don't have time to read the full text and want to get to the main point fast. The *anecdote lead* is for features, and tells a little story illustrating the theme of the larger article. The *quote lead* begins with a surprising, grab-'em-by-the-ears quote from a person being interviewed, or from interesting or unusual written material. I've seen quote leads using enticing descriptions of food from a menu; warnings of danger from a highway sign; and a shudder-producing death toll from a hospital report. The *echo lead* begins with a scene or quote that will be repeated, either in similar or exact words, tone, or situation, in the last paragraph of the story. The echo, or repeat, has ironic effect or emphasizes the point you made when you began.

There are a variety of takeoffs on these major types of leads. They illustrate how writers can be creative about the way they begin their stories, even in the more precise writing world of nonfiction. Fiction writers can use journalistic leads, molding them to fit the mood and theme of the story under construction. You can hook a reader with the promise of action, introduce a character, and hint at plot with a simple query or question lead. The important thing is that the question be exciting enough to make the reader want to know the answer.

Suppose your opening line is, "Now that we've only got two hours before the firing squad comes to get me, shall I tell you why I knifed Dolly?" The reader must yelp, "Yes! Yes! Tell me!"

HOW WILL IT END?

Many authors insist on knowing how the story will end before they start writing. In the previous chapter I said most writers are comfortable only if they can string their outlines on a beginning and an ending, like a hammock between two sturdy trees. Sometimes when you write the beginning, the end paragraph will come to you almost at once. If so, you're probably using some form of the *echo lead*. It's my favorite, because I know my ending will merely echo, or repeat, what I said at the beginning. It gives me a sense of completeness.

Some endings are inevitable; the reader knew it all along. Some are shockers. Some are ironic, making your point by a poetic twist of fate. Happy or sad, the ending must give the reader a gut feeling that the book is really over. Your character's life may go on, but his problem in *this* novel is resolved. You've said it all. Without that satisfying feeling of resolution, the reader is cheated and the writer is unfulfilled.

If you aren't happy with your beginning and/or ending, write some anyway. Write *something*. You can always go back and change your first words, or restructure the end on your second time around. Don't let imperfect first or last lines keep you idle for too long. You may need some time to begin with a bang. For now, just begin.

* * *

Set tone quickly, advises Dean Koontz. He started writing for the *Atlantic Monthly* when he was still in college, and went on to write over fifty novels and sixty short stories of science fiction, comedy, and suspense. He says writing is most successful when the tone, or mood, of a novel is part of its organization. This requires thought before writing.

"Set out the tone of your book right away. Will you write lean and spare? Lushly? Know the kinds of words you'll use, and the style with which you'll put them together. That will help you get started. And once you start with a certain tone, you must stick with it throughout the entire book.

"Never just sit down and say, 'I'm going to write a story about a cop and a killer.' You probably won't get away with that. You won't have a tone to the book or short story because you haven't thought it through enough. You must know the exact plot, the characters, what you're trying to say. Tone will come out of all those details, and so will organization. If you haven't done this kind of homework, you'll start down a lot of dead ends. If you're having trouble getting started, it's probably because you haven't worked out your tone, and you haven't worked out your tone because you haven't given it enough prior thought before you started to write."

Mood develops with first words, and lets the reader connect with the feelings you're trying to create in him. Paul Darcy Boles, veteran novelist and short story writer, says that his opening and closing lines are geared to manipulate the reader's emotions and put him in the mood Boles is in when he is writing that particular piece.

"I don't know my first sentence in advance, but I do know it must immediately set out the mood. 'He woke up fast' is my own favorite first line. Doesn't that set you up?

"The words for my ending might come about halfway through the story. The ending must say just the right thing, to leave you in exactly the proper mood. In *The Kid with Heart*, I end with 'He wanted to go on thinking about his father.' That's so the reader can go on thinking about the father, too.

"You can end a novel with the beginning of another story. A novel is usually open-ended; it has the feeling that life and people go on. A short story is a lightning flash that ends more distinctly because there are fewer characters to keep going on. The action can stop."

Start with suspense, suggests novelist/journalist Margaret Ann Barnes. Her powerful first book, *Murder in Coweta County,* recounts the bizarre but true story of a killing in rural Georgia. The book was fictionalized only in the spots where Barnes put words in the mouths of characters who were already dead when she began writing. To overcome the inevitability of the story's ending, Barnes began with a buildup of suspense.

"The beginning of a book isn't easy. I had to think through my first paragraphs for a long time, then try out seven or eight different ones before I got it right. I aimed for suspense. I was writing a true story where everybody knew the outcome [so] I had to give it life and mystery. I ended up with this first paragraph: 'Wilson Turner was doomed. Without benefit of a trial, judge, or jury, he was going to die. Turner was certain of it. The only uncertainty was *when*.'

"Turner wasn't my main character. All the textbooks tell you to start with your main character, but I started with a man I was going to kill off in a few pages. It was the only way the reader would really get into what happened to him. I wanted readers to feel the desperation of a man facing inevitable death.

"It does help a lot if you know what you want your readers to feel when they read those opening lines. And the same goes for the ending. I thought about it and decided I wanted to leave the reader with a reflection of my hero, the sheriff, as he normally was. I wanted the reader to see that his life went on. So I ended with him going out on another case. It was the best way, I thought, to leave the reader in a life-goes-on mood."

Start and stop with action for fast-paced thrillers
of the sort written by Bill Diehl. Diehl packs an amazing amount of events into each book, so he has to start fast, keep the pace going, and end with a satisfactory resolution of the conflict.

"My first line is calculated to grab the reader. What I write first doesn't always end up as the first sentence, but what always does happen is that the action takes place very fast.

"One way to dive right in is with detailed descriptions of something scary. When I start with a guy going into a drugstore to buy the medical implements with which he will kill instantly, I name every name, give every scary detail. Later on, when I might be writing descriptions that I want for poetic effect, I don't have to go into such precise detail. But that detail—detail of lots of action to keep up the tone of the book—is a great way to begin and end."

Slow beginnings can work, especially if you want
to coax the reader into your book with poetic descriptions, not shove him in with action. Tom Cook does this when he works on what he calls "symbolic" novels. They start with a deliberately slow pace, perhaps with a main character musing about his past.

"I like slow beginnings, so I enjoy reading and writing novels with detailed descriptions of places, or the thoughts on a person's mind as he begins or ends his day. I think these slow beginnings build the book. Look at the work of the great masters. You'll see they started slow.

"My endings are usually written by the first third of the

book. It can end with a climactic scene; that's a 'bang' ending. For a more serious novel, I like to end with the main character coming to a full realization of the idea he symbolizes. It's an intellectual resolution. Then a kind of peace settles in. I think the serious reader—my kind of reader, I hope—seeks this kind of peace. He can find it in slow beginnings and endings."

Start each chapter with action. That's the advice of novelist Robert Newton Peck. He says readers might tire of your book along the way if you don't treat each chapter like a new beginning.

"Each chapter *is* a new beginning. It must hook the reader with action words and short, snappy paragraphs. Big paragraphs of descriptive narrative turn readers off. Slam-bang chapter openings with lots of action keep them racing through your book.

"Open any of my novels to any chapter and examine the chapter openings. Usually my first paragraph is composed not only of one line, but of very few words. Here are a few examples: 'He is dead, sir.' 'The rum is gone.' Often my first paragraph is less than a half line long.

"And that paragraph is always physical and immediate. Someone is talking about something important. It pulls the reader right through the book. That's the function of lots of good beginnings—lots of good chapter beginnings.

"The end wraps it all up and slams the door, but not too hard. You want people to realize that you'll be back again. If you have a good end chapter, with a 'sock'em' last paragraph, readers will be looking for your next book on the store shelves."

Think out your ending, as does writer Anne Rivers Siddons. Her intricate novels, like *Fox's Earth*, sometimes take years of thought before even an outline is put on paper. A fixed ending is always part of that outline.

"I always know what my ending is before I put down the first sentence. Sometimes I even know the exact words. Perhaps I start backwards, with the ending firm in my mind before anything else. That's because I want the ending to make a statement, to wrap up the theme of the entire work.

"Often my characters change during the course of writing a novel—it takes years—but the ending is solid. It's fixed. I have enough sense of my main character when I start to know that even if he does change a bit, his ultimate fate, his last act, is sealed. And that ultimate act must never be inconsistent with the character's personality. It can be a surprise, even a shock, to the reader. But you must be sure the character has shown himself capable of ending up as he does."

Editors want to be hooked, just like readers, says senior editor Larry Ashmead of Harper & Row. That's why your novel's first lines are so important in helping to sell the book. Editors may help established writers devise those "hook 'em" beginnings. But if an editor is unfamiliar with your work, you need good first lines to lure him into reading your full manuscript.

"The beginning should always hook the reader immediately. The end should tie up things. You have to snag your reader right on the first page. People browse in a bookstore and start reading, and they'll go on and buy the book if the first page hooks them. The starting writer must hook the reader and the editor on page one. Of course you'll have to get the editor first, or you'll never be published.

"As for endings, they depend a lot on the type of book you're doing. Mystery or suspense novels can save the punch for the last paragraph. But if it's other than mystery, the 'ending' is the whole last chapter. It has to satisfy everything the reader wonders about."

Opening lines can change, so don't worry if your first few paragraphs don't thrill you as much as you think they should. They can be revised and rewritten later, or changed by an editor. *Chiefs* author Stuart Woods feels that if beginners have a good plot, characters, and style, a sympathetic editor can teach them how to overcome their weak opening or closing lines.

"Writing teachers put an enormous amount of importance on first lines and last paragraphs, so I labored over those very hard. Despite all that hard work, later on chapter one became chapter three! So that taught me you can ease into your book. Your first lines needn't be that captivating. If they fall down hard and the rest of the story stands up well, an editor can help.

"My first lines turned out all right after all. Still, my editor suggested a prologue, so *that* really became the beginning of the book. The prologue started the tension and moved it right into chapter one. It was a good change.

"I ended with one of my characters brooding over his lost youth. He was an overview character who didn't figure deeply in the plot but served to pull things together. It seemed natural for me to end with him. So, that's what I did. If I ever got stuck on a beginning or end, I'd trust my editor to help me think things through so I could find my way."

Stick to believable beginnings, to make sure readers can identify with what's going on. Pat Golbitz, senior editor at William Morrow, warns novelists to stay away from big "headline" stories that seem like appealing opening material for a novel, but which may strain a reader's ability or willingness to go with the rest of the story.

"When hundreds of people drank poison Kool-Aid in the jungles in obedience to their cult leader, many novelists thought, 'Wow, what a novel that would make!' But they were wrong. After such a beginning, where can you go? Even if the story was true—which to the best of our knowledge it was—it was beyond our common experience. Thus, it's not good book material.

"The Jean Harris trial, on the other hand, has many good opening possibilities and translates well into fiction. You don't have to stick to facts; facts are the adornment of a novel. If your way of getting ideas for fiction is to read newspaper headlines, watch for stories with which ordinary people can identify. Good beginnings and endings come naturally out of that."

Start with questions; end with answers, says Frances Statham. She writes historical romance novels that immediately arouse reader curiosity with direct or implied questions. The questions set up a scene, hint at a plot, and suggest character—and it all happens almost at once. The beginning of a novel poses a question and the ending must answer it, says Statham.

"Essentially, I start all my stories with a 'what-if' question. 'What if' a man sold his own wife as a slave? The question places you in a time frame—the days of slavery—and it's an interesting enough question the reader will want to go on and figure out how it can be done. So the opening, to me, is the what-if game.

"You go through the great middle of the book showing how the game is played out. Then the ending is the final resolution of the game, the final answering of the big question posed up front. It's all very neat if you think about it and know the question and answer in advance, and how the action will evolve."

Don't drag out the ending! You are writing a book because you have something to say, exclaims *Atlanta Journal-*

Constitution book review editor Michelle Ross. So, the ending should *say* it. Ross reads about four books a week, writes reviews, and interviews many writers. She says successful novelists aren't afraid to end with a bang, and claims that vague, "dribble out" endings annoy readers.

"If you're a reader being told a story, it's human nature to want to know how it all turns out. The most popular exception is *Gone With the Wind*. But endings that leave the reader wondering what happens are becoming less and less popular. For example, I'm getting tired of the *New Yorker* type of ending where a vague impression of time is captured in a short story. There's a mood there, an impressionistic quality, but it's irritating to me. I want an ending to have more substance. That doesn't necessarily mean something concrete has to happen; a death, a birth, a resolution. It means I want to feel the writer really had something to say when he started the book—and that the ending said it."

8 | Keep Your Fiction Flowing

YOUR BEGINNING SPARKLES; the end comes like an earthquake. Great. But how do you keep readers from being bored in the middle of your book?

This is a dual problem of craft and endurance. Craft is knowing the various writing techniques such as viewpoint and flashback, and being able to use them effectively to hold the plot together and keep characters in line. Craft is learned in writing schools and workshops, and from detailed analysis of fine works.

Endurance is the physical and emotional strength you need to keep fiction flowing. The grace and impact of your work depends largely on your ability to follow the advice of writer Celestine Sibley: "If you try for precision, if you say exactly what happened, you can avoid being sentimental and silly in your writing . . . When you're moved by something, you write moved."

STAYING AT TOP SPEED

Writing emotion is hard. It's exhausting to keep up the emotion that fuels fiction. If your work is to be exciting, you must be *excited* every moment you write; no wonder many authors exclaim they lose weight, wreck marriages, or guzzle booze during the course of writing a novel. Their emotional motors are always running at top speed.

Many writers produce the mood they need for a scene by recalling the fury or peace of a certain time in their lives. Memories spark the proper emotion, and the writer gets it down on paper while he's "hot." Later he can go back and edit words or rearrange sequences, but the captured power of true feelings remains.

Too many beginners waste time searching for fancy words or experimenting with style. But experienced writers almost all have the same thing to say about the best way to zip through the middle of a book: keep it simple.

FILM-THINK

Many novelists say they think in terms of films to make their fiction flow. This works well in describing the passage of time. Study films; they *show* time passing. They don't *say* it. In many old films a wildly flipping calendar illustrates a span of months or years. A field of flowers would change to one covered by snow, to show the passage of seasons. In writing, all this can be put into words. For example, you can describe the graceful hand of a young girl as she admires her new engagement ring. Then you can show how the hand grows gnarled and wrinkled, but the cherished ring is kept polished and is still admired.

CUT THE BLAB

Screen dialogue also helps writers keep the words of their

characters brief and succinct. Alan Armer, who has written, directed, or produced more than three hundred television programs and is the winner of an Emmy award, says the dialogue in most novels won't stand the test of being read out loud. Scriptwriters have to do that, and it saves their characters from a lot of useless blabbing. Reading your work out loud—acting the part—also forces writers to keep dialogue believable. You'll *hear* anything that sounds silly.

In fiction, characters don't always express emotion with their own words. Maybe your hero, Bill, just had a fight with his girlfriend. She saunters away with another guy, and Bill snarls, "You bitch!" The reader knows Bill is mad, but that's not enough. You must describe his feelings more precisely, even if Bill can't articulate them right now. According to novelist R.V. Cassill, the art of telling the reader why the character feels as he does is called "rendering." You render the feeling understandable by getting inside the character's mind. You might say of Bill: "He saw her walk away with Jack, her small round ass mocking him, bouncing further and further down the block, making his lust turn to simmering disgust." Bill is more than mad; he is also humiliated and disgusted, and his girlfriend's rear end is a good focus for these swirling emotions. Cassill says "rendering" makes emotions real, preparing the reader for a smooth slide into what happens next.

MAKING READERS WORK

Not all techniques are devised to give readers that smooth slide. Good writers demand good readers; they make the audience work hard. One of my favorite examples of this is Russell Hoban's futuristic novel, *Riddley Walker*. Riddley is twelve years old and lives in "Inland" (England), long after "Bad Time" (a nuclear holocaust). He speaks in a garbled folk language that sparkles with double meanings and emotional thunderbolts. Riddley's people are aware that computers were once important; they say of a man who went crazy that "his numbers all gone randem and his program come unstuck. . . ." They pray to a god as "Thine the han what shapit the black. . . ." And they whisper of the power of the atom, referring to it as "The Littl Shynin Man the Addom."

Hoban has a lot of guts to create such a language, spoken by deeply thoughtful survivors of some terrible big bang that the reader must re-create in his own mind. Hoban certainly doesn't make things easy for readers. His technique is to make them sweat over each word, pulling out its meaning and fitting it into the author's tale in a way that makes the most sense for you. But considerable thought went into writing *Riddley Walker*, so why shouldn't that same thought go into reading it? If you can pull off a technique like Hoban's, rewarding the hardworking reader with a new way of looking at the world, it's worth the sweat on both sides.

Harriet Adams was another writer who did not believe in making things too easy for readers. "Adams" was a pen name for Carolyn Keene, the late author of the Nancy Drew stories written for adolescents. These stories are a good deal more down-to-earth than Hoban's, but they share one important rule: Never talk down to the reader. Adams was never afraid to use big words in her books. That doesn't mean she threw them in just to force kids to the dictionary. She used pandemonium when that's just what she meant; if the reader had to look it up and learn something new, so much the better. This is not inconsistent with simplicity. Neither Hoban nor Adams made characters think in circles, contorted sentences, or strained for complex words when small ones would do. The trick is to be simple, but not simpleminded, with your fiction. If the characters and the action have solid motivation—if there's a good reason behind it all—simplicity will shine through. The reader may have to work a little to understand what you're getting at, but everything should fall into place in a reasonable amount of time, and the reader will exclaim, "Of course! That makes sense!"

DOWN WITH DIRTY WORDS

A last reminder about one technique that doesn't make much sense anymore: dirty words. Many writers toss these four- and seven-letter adjectives into their fiction to spice things up. It doesn't work. Walter Kerr, drama critic for *The New York Times*, says dirty words are getting boring. Everybody uses them for everything, and the result is they express nothing. A writer who puts dirty words into the mouths of his characters too often does so because he can't think of other words to express anger, frustration, pain, or horror. This sort of writer, says Kerr, "is still the first kid on the block to say bleep. Here he is, patently dancing with glee or with the freshness, the invention, the courageous independence of it all. My question: where's he been?"

That's my question, too. I have no quarrel with a good dirty word in the right place. But like any other technique, when dirty words are used *just* for shock effect, *just* to jazz up an otherwise tedious plot or scene, they fall flat. It cheapens the writing and dulls any zip the words might otherwise have. Kerr says, "The words I'm talking about have become all-purpose substitutes, rushed in to fill every hole left in a sentence by increasingly lazy writers."

Enough said.

When enough is said, stop. That's what Kurt Vonnegut, author of *Slaughterhouse Five*, *Jailbird*, *Cat's Cradle* and other novels, tells writers. Vonnegut wrote tips on style for the International Paper Company, making a special point of not rambling, to keep things simple. He praised short sentences which stop when the thought is expressed, instead of going on with frilly description. Vonnegut said that the two great masters of language, William Shakespeare and James Joyce, wrote sentences which were childlike in their simplicity. Yet the ideas were profound. "To be or not to be?" asks Shakespeare's

Hamlet. The longest word is three letters long. . . . The Bible opens with a sentence well within the writing skills of a lively fourteen-year-old; "In the beginning God created the heaven and the earth."

Don't tell the reader how to feel. *Make* him feel it, says Terry Kay. If you write that you feel a certain way, you're asking the reader to share the emotion—and he may not. But if you describe the scene that stirred the emotion in you, you're making the reader share the feeling because it becomes his own experience.

"Don't tell me how you feel. I don't want to read about you. I want to read a story about your character. Don't tell me that a sunset made you get all excited. Describe the sunset. Describe everything about it that made you feel a certain way, but stay out of the action yourself. Then, you'll make the reader experience what you experienced. You won't be telling him about it second-hand.

"Don't make the mistake of telling the reader how to feel. That's arrogant; readers won't obey. *Make* them feel. You have to do that, even though it's never easy."

"Fiction-Flow" comes with experience, Dean Koontz assures us. He claims he never met a professional writer who didn't admit that keeping fiction flowing page after page is a terrible chore. Koontz says most of the "pain and agony" of maintaining a flow comes from indecision. Since each scene can be done so many different ways, writers most slowly mature into the method by which they will exhibit their style.

"Keeping a steady course is so hard in fiction because there are a lot of techniques, and it's awfully confusing to figure out which ones work and which don't. Sometimes only experience teaches you, and what works for one writer may not work for another.

"I can only say what works for me. I don't use flashbacks; I think it's dangerous to dance back and forth between time frames. It really jolts the reader. Talking about the past can be done in very brief moments of reverie, or in conversations between characters. You can get stuck in a flashback for twenty or thirty pages, because you have to describe everything the character heard and saw and felt in the past. Take the essence of what you have to say and put it in your character's mouth. That takes one page. It's better.

"I also don't like the recent tendency to speak from two or three character's minds in one scene. It's sloppy to switch from viewpoint to viewpoint in one scene. It's caused by an eagerness to inform the reader about what different characters think. You don't need to know all points of view at once. Hold off. If Tom and Jane are fighting in one scene, you can tell it first from Tom's view, and let Jane have her say afterwards. Readers settle in on one viewpoint at the beginning of each scene, and you should let them stay there."

Paint pictures with little words, says Robert Newton Peck.

He writes about four novels a year and has completed thirty to date. In all of them, he says, his goal was to move the reader with the use of simple words strung together in emotional sentences.

"My technique—the thing that keeps my fiction flowing, I think—is to write with a camera, or paintbrush. By that I mean everything is a picture. First, I use little words: fire, not conflagration. War, not aggression. Then I try to show things instead of telling them. Instead of writing, 'The farmer had a horse, and he loved her very much,' I'd write, 'He lifted one split hoof, and bending low, stroked his mare gently to quiet the pain.'

"Writing is show biz. *Show* it."

Learn to use different techniques, advises Stuart Woods. He wrote light magazine pieces, humor, restaurant guides, a book on sailing, and a book on European hotels before he finished his novel, *Chiefs*. The technique he used in *Chiefs* was different from anything he'd tried before.

"I was in advertising for a long time before I decided to freelance, and that was good for giving me experience with lots of different styles. My most natural style is light and humorous. But I wrote my novel in a rather flat, declarative style: nothing poetic or lyrical. The description in the book is matter-of-fact, and I stayed away from lots of physical description because I think if you make suggestions about what a character looks like, the reader has a good time filling in the rest with his own imagination. For example, a very important character of mine is simply named 'Foxy.' I said he was called that because he resembled the animal. Let the reader imagine the sharp ears, the small eyes, the lean frame of the man.

"There are so many options open in fiction. That's why it's hard. You have to make a lot of choices. When I started my novel, all I really decided about how to keep it flowing was that I wanted to write in a style that would disappear into the story. I think if you get too style-conscious, strain too hard to keep that flow, the story will take second place. That's a bad choice."

Choose the order of your flow, suggests Damon Knight. That means tell the story in the order it happened. It keeps things simple.

"As a rule, it's best to choose the simple method of telling things in order. I hate flashbacks. They're inelegant. I know a lot of writers will disagree with me. But I think many people use flashbacks for no good reason.

"I also use the first person only when it's demanded, when it seems obvious that the main character must be the dominant voice. But I prefer third person. It's not difficult to keep your fiction flowing if you consciously stick to a very simple order of things."

Experiment with emotional language, recommends Anne Siddons.

In *Fox's Earth*, Siddons used a variety of phrases and sentences that she developed to evoke feelings rather than to inform.

"My sentences are made to conjure up images. That keeps things moving along because the images fit in with the mood of the story. One of my characters had a voice 'the texture and color of tepid water.'

"Now I know that voices have sound, not texture and color. But, remember, I wanted to fill the reader with emotion, not intellectual accuracy. I say a new baby is 'staring bluely' at her nurse. That evokes the blue-eyed stare that a newborn always has. And there is a 'dim, time-smelling old church.' If you think about it, time does have a smell: it's musty and rotten, and cold. But you don't have to think about it. You just have to *feel* it."

Feeling involves the reader, according to Art Spikol.

He writes columns on nonfiction for *Writer's Digest* magazine. In a 1981 column, Spikol says if you're writing fact or fancy, readers won't keep going unless you make them feel emotion.

"There's no law that a story has to unfold in any particular manner. But there is a law that it has to work; it has to read; it has to flow; it has to keep the reader involved . . . the present tense adds flavor, gives the tale immediacy, and makes the story seem less 'old.' You can also move back and forth from the past to the present. It's tricky; if you do it poorly, your reader will become sort of befuddled by the switching of tenses. But a good storyteller can weave in and out like that, from present to past to present. The past tense tells what happened, but the present tense may more effectively put us, the readers, into action. The past gives us some history; we can flash back to the protagonist's childhood, his family's eviction from their home during the Depression and his oath never to let that happen to him. The present has him moving down a street in the middle of a city forty-five years later, looking at a large stone doorway behind which is enough money to take him through the rest of his life. . . .

"A good storyteller knows how to get attention, inject a little suspense, exhibit a little of his character's character, and dangle a carrot."

Talk about emotions.
Then, you can more easily write about them, declares Frances Statham. She tells other writers to discuss human emotions and use what they learn from the discussions as a way to keep ideas flowing.

"The sharing of emotions—love, hate, sadness, loyalty, fear, vengeance—is the chain that links writer to reader. When the reader cares what happens to the character, and laughs and cries with him, the writer is on the right path. Flow comes naturally, then.

"Not long ago an English teacher told me many students have difficulty expressing emotion in their writing. They write, 'He felt sad,' or 'She was afraid.' That's not descriptive. I told her to talk about sadness or fear with her students. Discuss what personal fear does to the body: the rapid breathing, the cold sweating, the childish nightmare quality of being frozen to the spot and unable to escape.

"You can learn to do that. Discuss, and the discussion will translate into zippy writing. Soon it will become a habit, a good writer's habit, and you will have learned a new technique. I think it will inject maturity, smoothness, and confidence into your work."

Keep It Flowing

Confidence grows as you write. R.V. Cassill urges writers to keep a record of what he calls their "new maturity." He says it will turn into another technique to maintain the flow of words.

"As you write, your philosophy will grow and evolve. It should. Expect to change while you're writing, and expect the writing to change along with you. Keep a record of this change. It should be in the form of a notebook—a second book, if you will—in which you record ideas, philosophy, bits and pieces of dialogue you heard or imagined, and new techniques you've dreamed up. Review this notebook each day before you continue writing. It may pull you off course, but the new course may be better. You may find a new voice."

"Voice" of a novel is a selling point which lures publishers. Tom Cook believes sample chapters of his novels interest editors partly because it's easy to tell at once how they'll be written: as mystery, comedy, romance, or in a philosophical vein. He says finding a voice for fiction is a writer's first task.

"Once you find the novel's voice, its way of being written, the way you say things, half of the work is done. The voice should be established in the first sentence and the writing must not depart from the mood of that sentence. I start one of my novels with the sentence, 'You cannot judge the nature of man by the way the sun rises at El Caliz.' Now you know that's not comedy or mystery. It will be introspective throughout. I think the ability to settle on a definite voice and stick to it is a pretty good definition of talent for fiction writing."

Street talk is a technique for Bill Diehl, who ventures out (sometimes with a tape recorder) just to be with people and listen to the way they talk. It helps his fiction, he emphasizes, if he absorbs the sights, sounds, and smells of real life instead of staying home.

"It's my technique to put down what people really say, the way they really talk. So I have to go and listen to people. I pay attention to their speech patterns. I hear the pauses.

"People use 'uh' and 'ya see?' and 'man!' and all sorts of little expressions to break up their sentences. Sometimes I tape-record this, but mostly I just listen and absorb. I've learned that people who are anxiety-ridden speak fast, and people who are fairly confident speak slowly. People who are trying to hold in anger go *very* slowly, and say every word with a sharp, menacing clarity.

"I drink in the speech, and the mood, and the dress, and the overall atmosphere of people and places. Then I go back home and put it on paper. Writing is a solitary profession, but if you stay alone too long you forget what people are really like. So you do have to get out there and hear the street talk.

"Also, being out with people and getting a real feel for them gives me confidence to try new techniques and experiment with ways to keep up the flow of my story. I always liked to hook readers very fast at the beginning, and I notice I'm going faster and faster in each new novel. In *Chameleon* my characters fall in love on one page, have an affair in the next three pages, and on the page after that he's preparing to kill her.

"This book started out to be about corporate greed. It changed into a diabolical thriller. It's very complex. The main character isn't introduced until the book is a third over, and the mystery is cleared up sixty pages before the end. One section is told in the first person, and another part is sort of blank verse, in paragraph form.

"I broke all the rules. Once you become a little successful, you aren't so afraid to do that. I wanted to stretch things, to try new techniques, new ways to keep it flowing. If you're confident enough, those experiments just may work. First, establish a flow. Then, keep it going so you can sell a few books. Soon it will be time to experiment with new ways to flow, new voices and techniques.

"It keeps things lively."

9 | Success with Short Stories

AMERICANS HAVE BEEN READING short stories for about one hundred forty years. They fell in love with the form in the mid-1840s, when Edgar Allan Poe wrote an essay defining short tales as thunderbolts of human awareness. Since then, the country's writers have labored to perfect the form. Short stories remain what must be the serious author's greatest challenge and joy.

In the 1920s, editors took great interest in short stories, encouraging writers like F. Scott Fitzgerald, William Faulkner, and J.P. Marquand to turn them out by the dozens. The *Saturday Evening Post* and *Collier's*, for example, often paid $4,000 for a single short story, and devoted forty-three pages to the form in one issue. The boom in shorts lasted until the mid-1950s. Then paperbacks and half-hour television shows lured readers away from short fiction, and the short fiction form slipped from our collective literary consciousness.

Now, however, short stories seem on their way to revived popularity. A new generation of short story writers is redefining the form, more magazines are publishing short fiction, and students are eager to learn its demanding techniques.

STARK REALISM

The short story in America is becoming more down-to-earth, using starkly realistic language. Straightforward, simply-told stories seem to attract more readers these days than stories which employ the weird twisting of words and ghostly quality of literary experimentation. Foreign stories, like those of Jorge Luis Borges of Argentina or Peter Handke of Austria, may have a surrealistic, almost bizarre quality to them. But Americans are a literal people, seemingly most comfortable with journalism, and thus they demand a blunt style much like reporting even in their fiction.

Some publishers will take chances with satire, fable, or parody; literary magazines will probably always provide an outlet for experimental literature. Donald Barthelme writes many unusual short stories for the *New Yorker*, proving that the large commercial magazines welcome excellent experimental short fiction. But the short story writers who are getting published these days for the most part imitate the terse, clean-cut journalistic style of Norman Mailer rather than the lingering poetry of Dickens.

THE POETRY OF FICTION

Short story writers are close cousins of poets, and good stories are often called long poems. Novelist Joyce Carol Oates says short fiction is "uncomfortably akin to poetry," reminding writers that shorts are difficult to write because, like poems, they are "a fragile clockwork in which a misplaced word or an injudicious cadence can ruin everything, and bring the entire structure tumbling down."

Few people are able to clearly define just what that structure is; even master storytellers apparently haven't figured out a formula for short fiction. Nobel prizewinner Isaac Bashevis Singer, whose stories are written in the Jewish folk language of Yiddish and translated into English, shrugs that he does not know the form of the short story. All he knows, says Singer, is that short story writers need a lot of experience and talent, because "the writer has to put into a few pages whole life stories with convincing plots and convincing characters." Singer insists that since space is so tight in a short story, it takes a near-perfect writer to produce one that is good.

SPOTLIGHT PEOPLE

Sewanee Review editor George Core gets more specific: he says short story writers do best when they make the people in the story much more important than narrative or plot. One master of characterization, says Core, is author Frank O'Connor. He uses simple speaking voices and deals with characters from every walk of life. Core says O'Connor's short stories shine because "his figures form a rich gallery of human conduct, of folly and foible, of hopeless whim and undefeatable expectation . . . baffled, decent people doing their best (and their worst) in the face of adversity."

The great Jewish writer Sholom Aleichem always puts people in the spotlight in his short stories. Many of these stories are drawn from familiar folktales of Jewish life, showing good-hearted humans caught up in the inevitable madness of politics, war, and the disruption of family routines. In each story, Aleichem's trick seems to be the sharp portrayal of character. Readers notice the individuality of a struggling father, a demented mother, or a confused child, while at the same time recognizing the universal truth in that person's life situation.

TEST YOUR TALENT

Putting great stress on character development in as few words as possible is one key to the successful short story. But there's no *set way* by which a writer must do that in a short story. And there's no specific group or school of short story writers in America today to whom one can point and say, "These folks are doing it right," or even, "This is the direction in which short story writing is going." Yes, clear and simple writing—the journalistic style—seems to be preferred. But that basic advice takes the short story in many different directions: into science fiction, mystery, romance, children's stories, stories for teens, and the "lifestyle" or "it happened to me" stories which seem most at home in women's slick magazines.

All of this gives short story writers a wide choice of subjects, characters, and markets, making short fiction a wonderful way for beginners to test their talent. There are some professionals who insist inexperienced writers will flounder if they try short stories, because the form is so exacting that it's almost impossible to avoid mistakes. Others, like Lawrence Block and mystery writer Judson Phillips, say they eased into novels by trying short stories first.

Block says it was hard, at the beginning, to keep up the prose narrative for even the 1500 words necessary to constitute a proper short-short story. But he gradually stretched his endurance—and his talent—and went on to novels. Phillips studied the short stories of greats like Dashiell Hammett and Ernest Hemingway and learned to cleanse his writing of almost all adverbs. Then he labored over ways to create short stories that would "provide something new, something of your own." He claims one reason why beginners should try short fiction is because if it doesn't sell, rejection won't be so agonizing.

"If you have a 60,000-word novel and it goes down the drain, it's a disaster; but if it's just a 5,000-word short story that is rejected, it's not so bad."

NEW WRITERS

There are new American writers like Donald Barthelme, Andre Dubus, and Ann Beattie who are beginning to shine in the world of short fiction. Dubus received an O. Henry Award in 1981 for a short story called "The Pitcher." Ann Beattie's collection of shorts, *Secrets and Surprises*, recently went into paperback. Other writers are seeing collections of their short stories being published by university presses, and educational groupings like *The Norton Anthology of Short Fiction* are enjoying success. New short story writers are popping up every day. But they appear to work rather independently. They are not part of a "movement" or "school" of short story specialists. Like the hundreds and perhaps thousands of unpublished or little-known writers who labor in their cubicles or at kitchen tables, they keep up a lonely but dedicated try at the short story.

WE KNOW YOU'RE THERE

We know those writers are out there. Hundreds of their best stories get into print in the *New Yorker*, *Redbook*, *The Atlantic*, *Esquire*, *Omni*, and other fine magazines. There are also seven hundred fifty literary or "little" magazines in America which encourage short story writers (even if they don't pay as much for their work) and publish as many of them as possible. Colleges and universities report overflow crowds in fiction and creative writing workshops; writing classes, short story workshops, seminars and lectures are flooded in almost any location where they are given.

Book publishers and commercial magazines, including the men's and women's slicks, mystery magazines, city magazines and even the weekly magazine inserts of some Sunday newspapers, seem convinced that more and more people want to read short stories these days. One cannot deny that a lot of people want to write them. So, there's great hope the short story will soon blossom again.

To help it along, you should know some of the practicalities of writing short fiction, such as manuscript preparation, markets, titles and mailing. You can find some tips—in addition to what you'll read here—in *The Beginning Writer's Answer Book* (by the editors of *Writer's Digest*); *Writing Fiction* (R.V. Cassill); and *Fiction Writer's Market* (Writer's Digest Books). *Chicago* magazine is also sponsoring a new Nelson Algren Award for writers of short stories between 2,500 and 10,000 words. The award is $5,000 and publication in the magazine. For information and deadline dates, which change every year, write the Nelson Algren Award, c/o *Chicago* magazine, 303 E. Wacker Dr., Chicago IL 60601.

* * *

How do you know whether to do a novel or a short story?

The complexity of the story will tell you what form it should take, says writer Louise Boggess. She is a former journalist who moved into short story writing in the late 1940s; she has done about twelve books and numerous stories since then.

"How do you know whether to do a novel or a short? When the problem is so complicated that you have two or three story angles to develop, you have a novel. When there's one idea, it's a short. A novel needs more characters and more plot development, and the setting has to play a greater role. That demands more detail.

"The time span is different, too. The short story covers about a week in a character's life, at the most. A novel usually covers at least six months.

"A novel [often] takes three plot lines: the romantic, the mystery, and the background or environmental line. Character conflict, action, and setting all play a part. In the short, you use one line only. Perhaps it's the romantic line. But you don't have the space for all three lines.

"People often get into a novel and fizzle out because they

realize they've only developed one aspect of an idea, and they're really writing a short story. Perhaps it will develop into a novel later. Beginners are *not* better off starting with shorts. It's a demanding technique that requires much condensation."

Shorts are more exciting than novels to Bill Diehl. And they may form the basis of a larger work, done in brief, fast-moving segments. Even if you've never published a short story, he says, you can write several of them, link them together, and come up with a novel.

"I tell a lot of short stories in my novels. One after the other, bam, bam, bam. I think that's how I get through these long writing projects. I never thought I'd be able to write a 700-page book until I realized that what I could do was flip out a string of short stories and tie them together. That's how I sustain a novel. It keeps me from getting bored with my own stuff, when I get near the end of a novel. My work doesn't show the strain of writing long pieces, but I show it; I look like a ghost when I'm done with a novel. I think I'd *be* a ghost if I couldn't think of it as a series of shorts."

Short stories make you sweat because the form is more exacting than novels, according to Truman Capote. He wrote short stories before he turned to novels. He told an interviewer years ago that his ultimate goal would be to perfect this form, because the short story presented such a difficult and enchanting challenge. Capote said the discipline imposed on him by short story writing taught him control and technique.

"Control is maintaining a stylistic and emotional upper hand over your material. Each story presents its own technical problems: rhythm, paragraphing, even punctuation. Finding the right form for your story is simply to realize the most natural way of telling the story. The test of whether or not a writer has divined the natural shape of his story is just this: after reading it, can you imagine it differently, or does it silence your imagination and seem to you absolute and final?"

Make one "absolute" statement in a short story, says fiction editor and short story writer Anita Shreve. In her *New York Times* article "The American Short Story: An Untold Tale," Shreve defined good short stories as tales which isolate one aspect of the human condition, coming full circle in exploring that aspect. Such tales, she said, do end with a definite, absolute statement the author wants to make about life.

"Like a poem, a great short story is often nothing more than an epiphany, a struck moment, a vision or an insight.

"But unlike many poems, the language of most short stories is immediately accessible; the relentless journey to the end allows the reader to experience a short, sharp shock of recognition. . . ."

Shreve said that *The New Yorker* receives a staggering fifty thousand unsolicited manuscripts each year. From these, editors select between none and five stories to be published. These stories come from what is commonly referred to as 'the slush pile.' Shreve says the poor quality of the prose is one explanation for the harsh statistics and the descriptive label of these piles of unsolicited short stories. The subject matter is another.

"At the moment [1981] there are a lot of hostage stories. Cat-killing stories, stories about children falling out of windows and college-Angst stories are also abundant. A disproportionately large number of stories end with 'Suddenly I woke up' or 'Suddenly I felt tired.' "

Success with Short Stories

Editors can sharpen style, remarks Jack Lange. So, if your adverbs (or any other words) need fixing, a good editor will help as long as he sees merit in your story. Style and wording of a short story are important, he notes, but most of all short story editors like Lange are looking for the unusual burst of human thought which a good short provides.

"There isn't that much room in city magazines for short fiction, so we editors do give shorts a pretty good once-over before we buy. First, I look for the obvious things: do I care about the characters? Is it well written and well constructed? If a short passes these tests, I really want the answer to the big question. Is what the story tells me worth knowing? That's what I call 'quality of thought.' I don't care what the subject is, and in many cases I can edit over the writing and help the author make it better. It's what the story tells me about life that's important."

Characters, mad or sane, are the most important elements in your story, declares R.V. Cassill. Cassill points to the short stories of Ernest Hemingway as marked reminders that people, not things, are what counts in most fiction.

"Nothing is more fundamental to creating a story than establishing a spatial, temporal environment and peopling it with human actors. Hemingway developed characters in their setting. In his short story about a soldier, Nick, we learn in three sentences the character's name, the bare beginning of characterization is given and we quickly learn that he has been wounded. He talks to the desperately wounded soldier sprawled in the sun next to him, even though the soldier cannot answer . . . Much of what we know and feel about people comes from watching them act in relation to others. In fiction our understanding of characters is deepened by action, plot, and complication."

Tired lines kill short stories, so take pains to avoid overused words and trite phrases. Readers might put up with these lines in novels but there's no room for them in short stories, says Gene-Gabriel Moore. He hosted a writer's television talk show, "By-Line," has interviewed over three hundred American authors, and writes books and short stories. He thinks that trite phrasing comes when the writer is so eager to get words on paper that he doesn't give enough thought to the concept of the short story before he puts down a word.

"A good writer has to prefigure a lot, whether he's doing a novel or a short. It may seem like a bore at first, but it's really a labor-saving device. In a short story, it will help save you from those worn-out plots and tired lines that are so tempting to use because they may be the first things that come to mind. In a novel, you have to figure out the nuts-and-bolts of your tale, the chronology, names and ages of characters, the events of the times. It should all be on paper before you start writing, so you don't get confused. If you get it on paper for a short story too, that's all the better.

"I write short stories because I think they're more serious than novels. And I do them because it's the writer's job to make the best of what he's got, the challenge to do the best you can in a short space. If what you're writing about is fashionable at the time, you'll sell. Television as much as anything determines what will sell, and what gets exhausted in novels and shorts.

"The Rodeo Drive novel is exhausted, I think, and so is the Indian novel and short story and anything about prehistoric tribes. The Chinese novel, and perhaps the mysterious Oriental short story, is coming. You can explore the theme at length in a novel if you know about the Orient or want to do a lot of research. In the short story your theme must be tighter, and you have to get right to it. Define your locale and character at once. And you'll be better off if you have a journalism background. Journalists write tighter."

131 Success with Short Stories

Try a writing trio. That's what journalist and author Len Teel did with his wife, Katy, and fellow newspaperman Ron Taylor. Teel acknowledges that his strict, nonfiction training taught him to write in the tight style demanded by short stories. Cooperation between journalists gave him the idea for a team approach to short story writing.

"I sit at my typewriter. Katy is at her typewriter. Ron sits on the sofa, holding his pipe in one hand and a book of quotes in the other. We write, and Ron's job is to keep us on track and organize the story.

"It's like a Quaker meeting. Anyone who has an idea for the next sentence just speaks up. We go a sentence at a time, and sometimes a word or a phrase at a time. In shorts every word counts, and you can't be slap-dash about what you're putting down. But you'll go nuts if you agonize too long over one word. We use a kitchen timer, and give ourselves twenty minutes to discuss an idea or a phrase or a word. When the bell rings something has to go down on paper. It probably will be edited later, but once in a while I'll put something down—anything—to move us off dead center. The person at the typewriter has the power to do this, so he has more force in the team. He also has more pressure, because it's up to him to get things down.

"We might complete a quarter of a page in twenty minutes, or do several half-pages in a series of twenty minute segments.

"I don't think a novel could be done this way, in segments, by a team. But for short stories it works well. We can labor over each word, and feel reasonably sure at the end of twenty minutes that we really put an hour into it, because three people were working during that twenty minutes. We can discuss phrases. One person can refer to the dictionary while another writes. We can share story ideas.

"I think the team approach to short story writing is a good way, especially for beginners, to learn the craft. It's always fun, and it's not lonely. We have only three firm rules: don't talk to anyone else about work in progress, don't show anything to editors without agreement from each of us, and split the costs—and the profit—three ways."

Short stories make money for Paul Darcy Boles, a longtime practitioner of the craft. In addition to many novels, articles, essays and book reviews, Boles has sold about one hundred fifty stories to top American and foreign magazines, and is now awaiting publication of his book of shorts. He says short stories have always paid best.

"I have always depended on short stories to keep me in money. I've written short stories when they were much in demand, and when the demand seemed to have dried up. I emphasize, 'seemed to,' because I don't think the short story is dead now, and it never will be. The markets aren't the same, but they're there, and they're big, and they'll continue to buy.

"I sold my first short to the *Saturday Evening Post* in 1958. This was after I'd already done four novels. My agent suggested I do shorts, saying there was good, fast money in them. He was right. I got $2,500 for my short, and it took a day to write it. I still get the same amount of money, and I still think it's good pay. Right after my first success with shorts I sold about fifty other stories to the *Post* and *Seventeen*, and to just about every other good fiction market in the country. In almost every case if you averaged it out, I made several thousand dollars for every two or three days of work. And the money came fast; the *Post*, for example, paid within seventy-two hours.

"I'm still selling, still getting the same pay, and still dedicated to the short story as an art form and as a way to make a good living. Extra money comes from second-sale rights, and when you're included in texts on literature and anthologies, and from foreign sales. It's possible to write some very decent short stories rapidly, for profit. The big markets like *Redbook* and *Esquire* are still offering at least $2,500 for each story. *Playboy* is even better, because they give you an extra $1,000 if you come up with their lead short story. *McCall's* and the *Ladies Home Journal* pay good prices for short fiction. So I must question good writers who say they can't make a living by writing shorts. I do. So can you."

Squeeze your story idea until every drop of meaning is clear. A good short story starts with a meaningful character, event, or situation, and renders a complicated idea as simple as possible. That's the definition of a short story according to Bill Emerson, former editor of the *Saturday Evening Post*. Emerson is a lover and student of the short story, having worked with short story writers for most of his life. From 1965 to 1969, he spent most of his time reading short fiction, and buying it for his magazine from writers—known and unknown—in the United States and from all over the world. He says one of the most important elements in a good short is the way it makes a point by boiling down complex human emotions to their simple outcome.

"The short story form is intriguing. One of its greatest arts is taking complexity and rendering it simple. I've bought short stories from many of the greats; I bought hundreds from John O'Hara alone. And why do I pick him as an example? Because he had a great economy of words and an ironic twist of mind. He could look at a very complex relationship between two people, for example, and answer the question, 'And what does this all mean in the end?' And he was able to tell that to the reader in just a few words. In doing so, he created a minor explosion of understanding.

"A short story editor—the one who buys—will ask himself, 'What is the impact of this story? What is the revelation?'

"I have always been more interested in the revelation than the description. I want the story to do something for me.

"I'll make a leap of faith and say all editors want pretty much that same thing too. With such an elegant and complicated art form as the short story, it's hard for any editor or writer to say he's an expert. But if I had to isolate three critical components of a good short story, I'd say they were suggestion, compression, and poetry.

"I know that's not very specific. But a lot of what you see in a short story is subjective. It boils down to: do I like it? You may think it's good fiction and I may think it's bad. It's a matter of taste.

"I have been an editor, a writer, and a teacher for a long time. I can only say that great fiction in the short story must evoke these words: vividness, wallop, artistry, impact. It's the way your art represents life; and, with its impact, the way your short story changes a little bit of someone's life."

Short stories endure, acknowledges Andre Dubus, whose work appears in magazines and book collections. In 1981 Dubus told *The New York Times* that short story writers have a better chance for a long career than do novelists, because short stories get published more frequently than do first novels. Dubus also likens the short story to poetry and insists that the story tells much more about life than does a novel.

"Our lives are not novels. They're a series of stories. That's how we talk to each other. I say, 'How're you doing?' and you tell me a story. Next time you tell me a different one. A life is a huge collection of short stories."

10 | Know (and Sell to) Thine Editor

AN EDITOR CAN BE your best friend. If he likes your work—and his boss lets him buy it—your editor may be in the right spot to help define and direct a lifelong writing career.

Good editors are writing coaches, cheerleaders, sales consultants, and long-distance buddies. They might have to convince a dubious publisher your work will sell, or that you're worth nurturing until it does. If you fail, your editor's job may be in jeopardy, but many editors are still willing to take financial and emotional risks for good writers. Writers who know and appreciate that can nurture relationships with editors that pay off in satisfaction and sales.

Relationships with editors are so important to some writers that many say they could not produce if their editors changed jobs, retired, or died. Others shrug that any editor will do, as long as the person is a writer's advocate and a competent wordsmith. Each writer-editor relationship is different;

the only common factor seems to be that writers insist on feeling at ease with the person designated as the editor. Note the word "designated"; most writers don't choose their editors. They are assigned.

EDITORS IN THE MIDDLE

Writers dream of deep, warm relationships with kindly editors. That can and does happen. But there are barriers to getting along. Editors are the employees of a publishing house, and writers sometimes get irritated because the editor appears to side more with the publisher. At a 1981 meeting of the American Writers Congress, it was decided that writers fight so much with publishers that they need a union for protection. Writers want to join forces to push for minimum contract clauses, increased royalties, free legal advice, travel grants, old-age pensions, and other benefits. Writer John Baker notes that American writers are "in an adversary relationship with publishers." Writers want better treatment and more pay; publishers scream about profits. Editors may get caught in the middle.

Another problem is that editors often don't live up to writers' visions of them as gentle, accepting pals. Instead, many editors are gruff, all-business types. Biographer A. Scott Berg says editors may appear cold and unreceptive to new writers because "they constantly have a financial gun to their heads." That gun may be forcing them to disregard new talent and hunt for big names. Simon & Schuster editor Jonathan Segal admits he needs profitable books of any sort to help finance more risky literary ventures. In 1976, for example, Segal depended on the $25,000 in profits he got for *Bodysculpture*, a how-to weight-lifting book for women, to offset money spent in publishing a first novel by Joseph Pintauro. The novel, *Cold Hands*, broke even. It got good notices, but sold only about forty-four hundred copies.

SALES AFFECT PROFESSIONAL RELATIONSHIPS

Still, Segal stuck with his new novelist. Other editors may be just as dedicated, despite depressed book sales and inflation that is pushing the average hardback price to about fourteen dollars. People will pay that much for nonfiction, but it's rare for an unknown novelist to command such prices.

Editors are also wary of taking chances on new authors because if they do buck the tide and support the author until he's famous, the author may then turn his back and rush into the arms of a richer publishing house. Henry Morrison, an author's agent, admits this: "It's a fact of life that sometimes an author abandons a good editor to make more money."

Still, editors are constantly on the lookout for promising authors. One way to find them is through the Editor's Book Award, which has recently been established for writers who haven't had a book published. The annual award, given to the deserving writer of an unpublished manuscript, is the idea of the Pushcart Press. If an editor endorses your work and regrets that his house can't publish it, ask him to nominate you for this award. If you win, Pushcart will publish your manuscript and you'll get $1,000 in prize money plus royalties. (Send the manuscript with editorial endorsement to the Editor's Book Award, Pushcart Press, Box 380, Wainscott NY 11975.)

GRIPES AND GRUMBLES

If an editor does agree to show your work to his boss, the publisher, and succeeds in getting it accepted, he may be rewarded with a series of gripes and grumbles from the writer. Writers complain that editors change words when it's not needed and miss words that do need changing. Editors are also blamed for failing to help keep track of sales and profits and neglecting the backlist book, although those chores often fall outside the editor's range of responsiblities. Writers accuse editors of buying manuscripts based on marketability instead of on the worth of the writer's talent, although it is the publisher—not the editor—who makes the final decision on what to buy. Often, a book is purchased because it happens to be in *fashion*, like 1982's books on dead cats, pigs, or preppies. Novelist Robert Olen Butler reports that his first book, *The Alleys of Eden*, was unfashionable when he wrote it and was turned down twenty times before Horizon Press took a chance on publication.

"From nearly all twenty rejecting publishers I received downright ecstatic letters [from editors] praising all the book's virtues except its marketability," said Butler.

Horizon's gamble worked. The book got rave reviews and is attracting the attention of movie companies.

Even experienced writers expect editors to insist on fancy book jackets and big publicity budgets; they don't realize that in a great many publishing houses the editorial department has little or no influence on marketing, promotion, or book design.

THE MUSIC OF AFFECTION

Some writers' complaints about editors are justified. Others seem just a way to let off steam; writing is a frustrating and lonely job, and editors are handy when you're looking for someone to blame when things go wrong.

But complaints seem to be only a small part of the writer-editor relationship. Some griping is inevitable, but a careful listener to a writer's conversation about his editor will hear the music of real affection among the discordant, complaining notes. Novelist Cynthia Freeman says her editor, Don Fine of Arbor House, invests at least one hundred fifty hours of telephone conversations, plus scores of letters, during the course of editing one of her novels. Pascal Covici, a great editor at the Viking Press, unselfishly labored to bring out the talent of John

Steinbeck by gently guiding his work, helping him through the breakup of several marriages, and even thwarting his own publishing house when other editors wanted to get rid of Steinbeck. Editor and publisher Robert Giroux made his reputation at Farrar, Straus and Giroux, Inc. by reading manuscripts late into the night and doing his best to charm both new and experienced writers. Poet Donald Hall tells this story: when Giroux first saw the legendary poet Ezra Pound, Pound didn't like the idea of meeting an editor without being forewarned. Giroux had unexpectedly popped into a luncheon. Pound glared at him and snarled, "What in hell are you doing here?" Giroux calmly replied, "I have come to pay homage to a poet." Pound got up and bowed to Giroux.

THE WHIPPING BOYS

Editors are also becoming the whipping boys for a lot of the book industry's problems. It's no secret that television and movies are doing better commercially than books, so publishers are eager to grab books that will translate easily into scripts. This may force editors to turn down fiction that isn't "visual." Francoise Brun-Cottan, of Big Stick Productions, sighs that descriptive, dramatic books get more attention these days than internal, lyrical ones, because the dramatic books make better movies.

"There seems to be an attempt to make things more visual, to conform to a structure people think we as moviemakers have to deal with," says Brun-Cottan. "Sometimes I wonder if publishing people consider it a defect when a book won't translate to film, and if that defect might even make the book unacceptable for publication."

It might. That's not the editor's fault, but some writers blame them anyway. One solution that writers have found is to seek publication by smaller publishing houses, which depend on book sales, not subsidiary rights, to make money.

SMALL HOUSES

Small book publishing houses offer individual attention to new authors, a chance to publish more "literary" work, and modest but usually steady profits. Small houses such as the Pushcart Press of Yonkers, New York; North Point Press of Berkeley, California; Peachtree Publishers of Atlanta, Georgia; and Apple-Wood Books of Cambridge, Massachusetts, have published successful novels, novellas, poems, and volumes of short stories. University presses sometimes also publish these, and often even *prefer* new, unpublished authors. Other small houses specialize in nonfiction or the work of regional authors. The houses are attracting more and more work of quality because they offer, among other advantages, the close attention of regionally-based editors. Many writers are delighted to form a relationship with a good editor who lives nearby.

FUN AT LUNCH

This delight is echoed by the editors, who say they're happy to be able to lunch frequently with writers, talk to them on the telephone without running up huge long-distance bills, and generally have the feeling that a friendly business relationship is forming at close range.

But having a good time at lunch certainly does not assure you of a book contract; editors don't keep their jobs by purchasing inferior work by people they happen to like. The friendship part of an editor-writer relationship comes in handy only if the editor likes your writing first, and you second. All other things being equal, editors prefer working with people they know and enjoy. It's safer and more fun than taking a chance on strangers. If you've shown that you are reliable, hand in manuscripts on time, produce consistently good writing and don't quibble over small points, the editor will probably want to do busines with you again and again instead of switching to someone he doesn't know. It's human nature to forge lasting bonds.

In the struggle to write, edit and publish good fiction, the need for that sort of relationship will never evaporate.

* * *

Editors must enjoy your work, admits Helen Elliott, editor and publisher at Peachtree Publishers. Elliot started her small house in 1977, simply because she loves books and wanted some way to give good regional writers an outlet close to home. The house did well with books of poetry and several humorous books by local authors before it graduated to novels. Elliott says she now gets at least one full-length manuscript every day—a lot for a small house. She makes her decisions about what to publish based on the quality of writing, strength of story line, opinions of her five in-house readers, and, most of all, what she likes to read.

"An editor will read something and let his subjective feelings take over. He decides to buy if he really enjoys reading the work, if he wants to stay up all night to finish the manuscript, if he just can't put it down. In that way an editor is just like any other reader. He doesn't think, 'Is this great literature?' He just thinks, 'Oh, I *like* this!'

"Of course, after the glow has died a little the editor takes a more careful, less subjective look at the writer's product. Does the writer know his subject, and does he understand the needs of the intended audience? Is the writing good and clear? We shy away from having to do too much editing. We'd work with a diamond in the rough, but much prefer a polished gem.

"There are many things the writer can do to enhance his chances with me or with any editor. First, let me admit that, being small, we work very closely with authors. There's no way to keep your distance. So if we don't get along—if we clash as personalities—I probably won't take you on.

"If we do get into serious talks about publishing your book, I like to see some glimmer of understanding on the writer's part about what it costs to publish a book. I don't want him to ask for the moon. I need to know he has some sympathy for the editor and publisher, and trusts them to do their best. One thing to remember is that it is inappropriate—and unprofessional—to try to dictate the design of a book or book jacket. A writer should concentrate on the story and the writing. Leave the jacket and book design to the publisher.

"If the manuscript comes by mail, you should include return postage if it has been unsolicited. We could just not send it back, but so far I'm reluctant to do that. The result is we spend a lot on postage, and that's a burden the untried writer should assume.

"Make your work as polished as possible before you let an editor see it. A lot of time you get only one chance at a house. There's so much an editor has to choose from that he's very reluctant to even bother with material containing mistakes in spelling or punctuation, or a manuscript that isn't neatly typed. You should also realize that busy editors would rather deal with a query and outline than a full-length manuscript. Include an intelligent letter with your package, telling the editor exacty what you intend to accomplish in your writing.

"It takes a short time to say 'no.' Saying 'yes' takes longer. Be patient. And if we do go ahead and decide to publish you, there's no guarantee of success. It's a roll of the dice; we take risks together. I'm willing to do that if I truly love your book. Then, I don't ask any questions. I'm behind you all the way and we win or lose as a team."

Avoid compromising integrity. Don't please an editor at the cost of sacrificing your own feelings, says novelist Frances Statham. She advises other writers not to write for the market but to follow their own inclinations and produce work of which they can be proud.

"An editor who wants you to write only what's in style is not a good editor. He doesn't have your best interests at heart; he's interested in the money. No writer should compromise

Know Thine Editor

his integrity like that. You don't need to bow to a selfish editor's whims to get published. It is *not* difficult to get published these days, despite everyone's cries to the contrary. I see new people getting published all the time.

"I find the inspiration first and the market second. If it's good I know I'll find an editor who likes it, so I write what interests me.

"When I finished my first book—I was a total unknown—I used the *Writer's Market* to pick out a potential publisher, then sent my manuscript to Ace. They used Gothics, and they were listed up front. Later, I got in with the William Morris Agency because I picked up the name in a creative writing class.

"One thing to remember in searching for your editor is that he or she will be more likely to pick up on you if your manuscript looks good. I do all my own typing, and if I cross out a word or a paragraph I re-type the whole page. When I revise, I re-type the manuscript—all of it. If I insert, I let the editor know pages are added by putting a little 'I' for 'Insert' next to the number of the page. So if I've added pages between numbers 223 and 224, for example, I'll make the new pages 223 I and 224 I and continue from there with the original numbering. I'd suggest using *The New York Times Manual of Style* or *The University of Chicago Press Manual of Style* for other ways to prepare a manuscript.

"Each editor has a different method and each publishing house does things a little differently. Ask! Most publishing houses have tip sheets, telling you how to prepare a manuscript and some of the tip sheets even tell you how to write the novel, going so far as dictating what the hero says to the heroine! I don't use that, but the material on the mechanics of putting the manuscript packet together can be helpful.

"I break up paragraphs and like a lot of white space on my paper. That's why dialogue is so good. Also, editors like to read it. They're really very human."

Being human, editors are drawn to personally addressed envelopes, advises Alan Williams of Viking Press. He tells new writers to send everything to a person, not just a publishing house. Get an editor's name from a friend or from a marketing book, and address the manuscript packet to him or her. That is the best way to make your story stand out from the hundreds of "manuscripts which flood in daily and are related to the 'slush pile.'

"That's not the way to get attention for your first novel. We publish very few books out of the slush pile, but the one we did recently turned out very well. It was *Ordinary People*. The paperback sold for $700,000 and of course it's a current movie. Very few good books go unpublished. If you get turned down by one editor, keep trying. Somebody, somewhere, will notice you."

Want to be noticed? Be businesslike when approaching potential editors, advises R.V. Cassill. It's essential to present a good manuscript packet that will trumpet your professionalism to an editor who doesn't know you. Cassill says a synopsis and neat package will help you make friends with editors through the mails.

"The synopsis is a summary. Use a strong opening paragraph that tells the story line and philosophy behind your novel. An example might be, 'This is a story about an evil mother who abuses and betrays her daughter and is wounded and abandoned by the daughter in her old age. The philosopy is that the bonds of parenthood are not sacred, and must be nurtured like any other relationship if they are to flower.'

"Include a brief letter telling about yourself and listing any previous publications. Then you need an outline of the story—it can be up to twenty pages—and at least two chapters. So your packet consists of the synopsis, outline, sample chapters, and cover letter.

Know Thine Editor

"All of this has to be on good white bond paper, 8½-by-11-inch, double-spaced in pica type, and very neat. Put the title of your novel about a third down on the first page. In the upper right hand corner of that page, start numbering the text. Also put down your name, address, phone [number], and the number of words you expect the final manuscript to run. Leave hefty margins (about one and a quarter inches on all sides), submit the original copy only (not a Xerox), and be sure to keep a carbon copy for yourself.

"Don't fold the manuscript. Place it, flat, in a manila envelope. Be sure to include return postage and a self-addressed return envelope (and hope it won't be used). With novels, you can send this same packet to as many editors as you can. This is in keeping with a businesslike approach. If you send you work to one editor at a time, you may wait months for a reply. Most writers can't afford the wait, either financially or emotionally. Sending the packet out to several editors at the same time saves you time, and time is money."

Money can destroy editor-writer relationships more than anything else, according to Sally Wendkos Olds, president of the American Society of Journalists and Authors. She said in a recent open letter to publishers that the members of her organization can barely afford to write books anymore because the pay is often very bad. Olds wants publishers to treat *writers* in a more businesslike mannner.

"The problem is that publishing has not become businesslike enough. A well-run business values its workers and pays them commensurate with their contributions . . . Writers who have been turning their skills to the writing of annual reports, corporate brochures, and executive speeches report that businesses pay better and faster than publishers do. Furthermore, in recognition of the fact that writers have day-to-day living expenses while they are working on a project, corporations almost always pay writers at least half of the agreed-upon fee at the time the assignment is granted, instead of making the writer wait until he or she is finished with a project before getting paid, as is customary in the publishing world."

Get paid as you write. You can do this by selling "partials" instead of full manuscripts. San Diego writer Chet Cunningham overcame money problems and made friends with Tower Publications editor Susan Calderella in New York by writing "partials." When Calderella asked Cunningham to split his proposed 180,000-word novel into three 60,000-word books, he obliged by sending her part of each manuscript instead of tackling three new books at the same time. That was in 1976. Cunningham has since sold forty-nine books, most on the "partial" basis. He wrote about his technique in *Writer's Digest* magazine, telling other writers that "a partial is simply 'short stopping' the novel about a quarter of the way through, after the story idea, people, themes, and plot outline have been created. The writer sets out the first five or six chapters, polishes the rest of a chapter-by-chapter outline and presents the package to a publisher as a marketable product. Cunningham says such partials take about a month for him to do in comparison to spending years on a full novel.

"An experienced editor can look at this much of a novel and know if it will work as a book and sell for that house . . . The beauty of working with partials is that when you sell one, you sign a contract and you get half the advance. This is the pay-as-you-write plan, one of the best basic reasons writers try to get a book contracted before it is written. They don't waste time writing a book that won't sell, and, more importantly, they get half the advance to help finance the grocery bills while they're writing [the remainder of] the epic."

Be businesslike in dealing with editors. It's the

best way to begin and maintain a healthy working relationship with editors, says freelance editor Barbara O'Brien. She has edited about twenty-five books and worked with many writers in her six years as an in-house and freelance editor; she feels that friendship is nice but business comes first.

"So many amateur writers approach editors with chips on their shoulders, convinced that the editor is the enemy. Either that, or they think he's a substitute for their daddy and is there to gossip and play. It's always helpful to let the writer see the publishing business through the editor's eyes from time to time.

"The writer needs to keep in mind that the editor is an employee of the publisher and is not all-powerful, not even within the company he/she works for. The actual influence the editor has on the book's marketing and promotion, for instance, varies from publisher to publisher.

"I cannot stress enough that a writer must have a professional attitude toward his work and toward his editor. Some editors and authors do get chummy, but most editors I know just love stick-to-business writers. Editors are nearly always swamped with too much work and don't have time for lingering lunches and witty chats on the phone.

"The biggest technical problem writers have is with structure and chapter-by-chapter organization. Editors spend a lot of time shuffling things around so the author's work will make sense. This mechanical work takes time and patience, and it helps if the author stays as objective as possible about the procedure. We respect the emotional stake a writer has in his creation, but it's no good if that creation is too disorganized for a reader to comprehend. The editor is often responsible for a tightly-knit, well-organized book. It is the editor who probably has done the knitting. Stay businesslike and help him out with it. Perhaps all you will need to do is show faith in his judgment and not scream if things get changed around. The editor will appreciate your mature attitude."

Ask a pal to help you get acquainted with an editor, says novelist Anne Rivers Siddons. She tells unknown writers to find a friend who is a published writer, and get introduced to his or her editor.

"That's one reason why it's important to have friends and acquaintances who also write. It's not easy, but if you have a trusted friend who is an accepted author, ask your pal to introduce you to his editor. Go to New York or wherever that editor is, and meet him or her personally. I think that's the best way for a new writer-editor relationship to begin. If I had a manuscript and didn't know what to do with it to get it published, I'd turn to a published writer who was willing to tell me what editor to go to. That writer, however, must have read your work and liked it; you really can't ask for an introduction unless there's professional merit, not just friendship, behind it.

The next best thing is having an agent. The agent will function as your friend. Agents are pros who know what editor is looking for what manuscript. I couldn't get along without my agent.

"It's not easy to find a published writer and make friends, and of course it's not easy to get an agent, either. But of the two I think it's easier to make a friend. I call it 'networking'; businesspeople do it, and writers should too. It's really helping one another. So worry about agents later. Make friends first. If you succeed, you'll have both a new friend and an editor."

Love 'em, buy 'em, leave 'em. That's what some editors do to writers. The editor may court you, buy your work, then ignore you, laments Robert Giroux, editor and chairman of the publishing firm of Farrar, Straus & Giroux. In the 1981 Ninth Annual Richard Rogers Bowker Memorial Lecture, delivered in New York City, Giroux explained that some editors may function only as talent scouts. Once they find a good writer they too often turn him over to another editor, and there's little time to develop a lasting relationship.

"The acquiring editor frequently signs up books before they are written, and often has no time to read them after they are written, since he is busy landing his newest acquisition. Perhaps the acquiring editor feels no need to read; it's names and reputations he's after . . . The traditional function of the editor as the author's close collaborator from manuscript to printed book, and through all the aftermath, has too often been neglected, with deplorable consequences, in the current atmosphere of heightened commercial pressures and a largely acquisitive publishing posture. Editors used to be known by their authors. Now some of them are known by their restaurants."

Editors can dump writers after the book is published, too. That's a sad reality many writers don't like to face, according to Cliff Graubart, owner of Atlanta's Old New York Book Shop.

"If an editor really likes your book he can often prod the promotion department to give it a lot of play. It's the advertising that sells a book; no matter how great your talent, the book probably won't fly unless the promotion department of your publishing house *makes* it fly with a big advertising budget.

"The editor can influence that. He can agitate for you. But too many times he won't lift a finger, and there goes your book down the toilet. There are just so many ad dollars to go around, and there are lots of books in each publishing house competing for those dollars. Each editor is working with several writers. He'll try to get those ad dollars for one of *his* writers; he'll fight for you if he's so inclined. If not, he'll dump you and turn his attention to another writer whose work—or company—he favors. That means he edits you, then forgets you.

"You can find out how hard the publishing house will push your book by finding out how many copies they'll print.

If they print less than eight thousand, you can't expect much more than one ad in your local newspaper. The publisher just doesn't have that much of a stake in getting the book sold. He can write you off as a tax credit. If, say, 30,000 copies are being printed, the publisher *has* to put on an ad blitz. The house can't sit on those many books. So ask your editor, 'How many books are they publishing?' The answer will tell you how much the editor and the publisher really love your work and how hard they intend to promote it.

"The writer gives his all to a book. Then he turns it over to an editor and by and large it's out of the writer's hands. The editor, with the publisher, calls the shots from then on. Oh, he'll tell you sweet things while you're writing; he'll say you're great and encourage you to keep on going. But when you're done, what happens next is up to him. There's very little a writer can do to influence book sales, and thus his own career, except [to] please the editor enough with quality and personality so the editor will push for those big promotion bucks."

Good editors are rare.
Many of them job-hop so frequently they don't have time to forge close ties with writers. Or, they are so pressed for time and money they may do little more than tinker with your work, then rush on to the next mechanical chore. Gene-Gabriel Moore, author and book critic, believes close relationships between editors and writers (the "days of Maxwell Perkins," as he calls them) are mostly gone.

"For writers everywhere, the promise of being published and satisfactorily rewarded for that publication grows dimmer each day. That's partly because publishing houses are no longer family-owned, but run by huge conglomerates. A conglomerate isn't filled with the kinds of editors—the legendary Max Perkinses of the world—who brought honor and worth to American letters. They are run by accountants and efficiency experts and computer specialists and authorities on profit-and-loss sheets.

"I don't mean to be unnecessarily gloomy, but writers must live with these facts. One of the reasons you'll see small houses like Peachtree Publishers grow beyond a regional posture is that they take chances on the small book, not just the formula blockbuster.

"When and if you find a good editor, hang on for dear life. Don't think for a minute the publisher has the writer's best interests at heart. Publishers think money. Editors do too, but not to such a great extent; they still spring from a background of advocacy for the writer.

"When you sign a book contract you usually sign away all control of your work to a publisher. Publishers are in trouble, so editors are rushed and harried, and writers suffer. The only way to gain protection is for writers to unite in a union. It won't thrill publishers, but I would imagine a good editor would welcome an organization that helps writers."

Sensible suggestions come from editors, remarks Stuart Woods. He says part of the editor's job is to give the writer ideas about how to make the manuscript better. Woods and his editor at Norton Books disagree now and then, but most of the time Woods accepts his editor's advice. He moves scenes and chapters around as his editor suggests.

"I'm receptive to sensible suggestions, and I think any writer who balks at manuscript changes just for the sake of balking is never going to have a good editor-writer relationship. I have a great one. I always ask for my editor's reactions. I never call up and say, 'Help, I'm stuck!' but I do always ask, after each chapter, 'Did you understand why the action worked out that way?'

"I talk to my editor two and three times a week. We've become close personal friends. He isn't a better writer than me—at least he doesn't tell me so—and he knows his work on my books can't be seen as more important than mine. He enjoys my work and wants to help, and to do so he has to be blunt, honest, and open with me.

"But my editor is also aware of how fragile a writer's ego can be. At the very beginning of our relationship, I had asked another writer to read my work. He wrote a letter to the editor saying how awful it was. He just crushed my book. It bothered me terribly. This was a well-known author, and I couldn't get it off my mind for weeks. My editor soothed me by saying he didn't agree with the other writer, and that the letter grew out of jealousy. It made me feel much better.

"I intend to stay with this editor forever. If our relationship were ever severed, say by illness or death, I'd miss him terribly."

Editors move around, warns fiction and nonfiction writer Kim Chapin. Chapin is the author of a book on tennis and one on stock car racing, and is now working on a novel.

"My editor at Dial Press, Juris Jurjevics, told me he'd take a chance on financing my first novel, and forked over $16,000 in advance money for an untitled, uncharted book.

"I know it will have a vague stock car racing background, but the rest of the novel is a mystery to me. I also know I'm extrordinarily lucky to have formed a relationship with an editor who will take a chance like that on an unknown novelist. But I try not to get too attached to him because I know editors part company with publishing houses at a startling rate.

"Ideally we would all like to go to one publishing house and spend our careers under the safe wing of one friendly house and one compassionate editor. But it doesn't usually work that way. The kind of relationship I have with my editor is nice, and it turned out lucky for me so far, but it's not the idealized long-term friendship you would imagine. Writers change editors and publishers all the time. Editors leave their jobs all the time. The whole publishing industry changes all the time. So you may well lose an editor with whom you've formed a great relationship.

"Some writers have contracts that say they must stay with the publishing house even if their editor moves on. That may happen to me. And I don't think Juris would be shattered if I took my second novel elsewhere. Also, I'll try not to be sad if he tells me I'd be better off with another publisher."

Be prepared to leave if your editor doesn't understand you or your work. Don't try to change a hostile or reluctant editor; the strain will stifle you both. Margaret Ann Barnes found that the Southern characters and subjects in her first book met with skepticism by Northern editors. She had to shop around for an editor who understood her Southern background and sympathized with the characters she wanted to portray.

"I had a terible marketing problem because I had written a Southern book with real-life Southern characters, and most Northern publishers refused to believe they were real people. I tried explaining that Southerners love eccentrics. In other parts of the country they don't put up with weird people; they put them in institutions. In the South we take care of them and write about them.

"My book read like a novel, but the people in it were real. Yet I had problems getting editors and publishers to believe that. They refused to believe my characters ever existed. I said, 'They're real. I can document it.' They only shrugged, 'So what? Nobody who reads the book will believe it anyway.'

"If you run up against a 'so what?' attitude, the relationship you're trying to forge just won't work. Don't try to force it. Wait until you find somebody whose chemistry clicks with yours. You'll be sorry if you grab the first publishing house, and the first editor, who shows an interest in you unless that house and editor are *right*. Before you sign a contract, be sure the interest will last. Then, you have a better chance that the editor-writer relationship will be a happy one."

11 | Agents, Contracts, and the Law

WRITERS HAVE ALWAYS BEEN on the front lines in the fight for freedom of expression. It's a dirty, expensive brawl—and it hits home every time you pick up a pen.

Will some editor steal your work? What's a copyright, and how do you get it? How do free press fights affect fiction writers?

Questions about law buzz around writers like an army of gnats, sapping creative energy and sometimes forcing retreat from the field. Recently there has been a societal swing in America to the sort of conservatism that opens the way for book banning—and burning—and encourages repressive laws that restrict writers, publishers, and book sellers. Agents and attorneys can help, but writers now cannot avoid assuming more of the burden of speaking up for First Amendment freedoms. We must push for our own legal protection.

NEAR V. MINNESOTA
One of the most famous fights for such protection came in

1926, with Jay Near's newspaper, the *Saturday Press*, in Minneapolis, Minnesota. This newspaper was a gloves-off rag that gloried in sensationalism; lawyers at the time called it "as malicious, scandalous, and defamatory as a paper could be." The paper ran afoul of a law that had been passed in 1925 to silence writers' attacks on politicians. The law was The Public Nuisance Act, and it had successfully killed another Minnesota newspaper, the *Rip-saw*.

Near wasn't about to see his paper also go down. He challenged the law in the famous *Near* v. *Minnesota* case, and won. It was a victory for freedom of the press and for writers all over the nation. More recently, the Near v. Minnesota case served as the foundation upon which the press relied for precedent in the Pentagon Papers case. Writer Fred Friendly wrote about Near's fight in his book, *Minnesota Rag*.

ATTACKS ON FREE PRESS

Through the years, laws in other states have tried to clamp shut the doors of the writer's freedom of expression. Attacks on so-called sexy books and magazines are fashionable these days, as the Moral Majority feels its oats. These attacks strike at all of us, forcing many fiction writers to defend their books and stories in court.

In Georgia, for example, the General Assembly recently passed a law banning the public display of magazines, books, or works of art deemed as sexually explicit. The law was supposed to be a way to keep kids from giggling over girlie magazines in the local drugstore. But it could result in people yanking everything from novels to sex education books off the shelves of bookstores and libraries. That could shut down plenty of authors, fast. Bookstore owners and local novelists such as Anne Rivers Siddons and Paul Darcy Boles fought hard against the bill, and others will have to join to keep the law from being enforced.

CURRENT OBSCENITY QUESTIONS

In New York, the Island Trees school board in Island Trees, Long Island, decided that high school and junior high school children shouldn't read certain fiction and nonfiction. So the board removed ten books from its libraries and curriculum, including *Slaughterhouse Five*, *The Naked Ape*, *A Hero Ain't Nothing But a Sandwich*, *Down These Mean Streets*, and *Soul on Ice*. A district court backed the board but an appeal court disagreed, and the U.S. Supreme Court will review the case.

The Colorado legislature is considering two bills to ban the sale of "obscene literature" to adults and children. If the bills become law, any time a customer in a bookstore browses through a novel and decides a passage is too sexy for his tastes, he can file a complaint with the police. Then the store owner and his lawyer must appear in court, or the store owner must strip the book from his shelves. One bookseller cried, "Authors stand to lose a great deal if laws like this are passed; why are they not involved in the fight?"

Good question. We can't huddle over our typewriters while the world outside savages our work. We'll have to become more legally educated and involved.

HELPFUL GROUPS

One way to do this is by making contact with author's groups which help writers learn about laws affecting them, find attorneys, and answer general contract questions. The groups may not be able to address your specific needs, but they often can steer you in the direction of finding a local group or lawyer who can. Some of these groups are:

The Author's League, W. Forty-fourth St., New York NY 10036. This is one of several national groups set up to provide information on royalty arrangements and advances, and to refer authors to competent attorneys or other authors' groups such as PEN (The Author's League) and CRAFTA (The Committee to Restore Artistic Freedom to Authors).

The American Law Institute, 4024 Chestnut St., Philadelphia, PA 19104, (215)243-1600.

American Legal Publications, Inc., 5 S. Buckhout St., Irvington-on-Hudson NY 10533. This group can be asked to refer authors to suitable reading material for further education.

American Society of Journalists and Authors, 1501 Broadway, Suite 1907, New York NY 10036, (212)997-0947.

GR & F Royalty Auditing Firm, 489 Fifth Ave., New York NY 10017. This is a private, for-profit group offering help in assuring that your publisher pays you the correct amount in royalties.

International Women's Writing Guild, Box 810, Gracie Station, New York NY 10028, (212)737-7536.

Libel Defense Resource Center, 30 Rockefeller Plaza, New York NY 10112, (212)265-3175.

Practising Law Institute, 810 Seventh Ave., New York NY 10019, (212)765-5700.

You can find other groups by asking writers in your home town. Also quiz the chamber of commerce, find out from university English or journalism departments, ask a librarian or a book shop owner, or scan the telephone directory.

GOOD LAWS

Membership in writers' groups will do more than help fight "bad" laws. It will keep you informed about good ones, too. In New York, for example, a bill has been introduced to shield writers from having to reveal their confidential sources of information. This is an extension of the same protection given to newspeople.

On the federal level, the U.S. Tax Court, in a suit brought by the *Encyclopedia Britannica*, ruled that prepublication expenses can be added to the ordinary deductible cost of publishing a book instead of having to be capitalized over the years. Also, authors can now deduct book-writing expenses in the year in which the expenses are incurred.

KNOW LIBEL LAWS

It pays to keep track of these laws, both bad and good. It might help the rest of us from falling into the same sort of mess that recently engulfed writer Philip Cioffari, who wrote a short story for *Penthouse* magazine. In the story, Cioffari made fun of a beauty pageant, depicting a brainless beauty from Wyoming who has sex with several men while she's a contestant in a Miss America contest.

A real Miss Wyoming, who represented her state in the 1978 pageant, was horrified enough by the story to sue Cioffari and the magazine for libel and invasion of privacy. The court ruled that the woman was, indeed, defamed by the story, awarding her $14 million. The size of the award stunned writers and publishers and spurred the Author's League to challenge the judgment in a U.S. Court of Appeals.

The basis of the challenge, according to the League, is that anything written in a short story or novel can't be libelous if a reasonably intelligent reader realizes it is written as fiction. Furthermore, the amount of money demanded of Cioffari and *Penthouse* would have the effect of scaring other writers and publishers into silence.

A lot of people are already scared. So many writers have been sued lately that they're demanding some form of liability insurance from publishers. The first to respond has been Viking Penguin. In January of 1982, the house insured its authors against losses from libel, plagiarism, invasion of privacy, and other legal sorrows. Other publishers are reportedly interested in doing the same.

LEGAL SELF-DEFENSE

Writers are also becoming adept at practicing legal self-defense. Ken Lizotte, with a contract to write scripts for a management training company, worked for the company for almost two years before his contract ran out. Ordinarily, a writer out of work isn't entitled to unemployment compensation. But Lizotte pressed the issue in his home state of Massachusetts, and won.

Author Michael Major sends potential publishers his own contract. He's had good luck in getting people to sign on his terms, or at least to consider many of his demands. Major asks for payment on acceptance for stories instead of payment on publication, among other considerations. Once editors get over the shock of seeing a contract by an author, they apparently respond well. The American Society of Authors and Journalists provides members with sample contracts they can use or modify to fit individual needs.

BEING REASONABLE AIDS SUCCESS

One key to success with the law is being reasonable, like Major. One author who apparently went too far in her demands on a publisher found herself on the losing end of a suit.

This author sued her publisher, because, she said, her book was inappropriately titled and contained many typographical errors. In her anger over these mistakes, the author sent letters to libraries calling the publisher a fraud. She also said the Princeton University Library was "harboring stolen goods" because it kept the book on its shelves over the author's objections. To top things off, the author had a policeman serve a criminal summons on the publisher.

Apparently, a judge thought the author went too far. He said the author's conduct toward her publisher "might raise a question as to her right to equitable relief." He ruled against the author.

Writers may feel that dealing with the intricacies of the law is an unfair burden. But there seems to be no escape; like other businesspeople, we writers must pick our way through society's legal jungle. It is filled with hungry, censoring beasts. With the help of agents, attorneys, and our own knowledge and common sense, we can avoid being devoured along the way.

* * *

Cruel testimony from enemies of people about whom you're writing can get you into trouble, warns Kitty Kelley. She is the author of *Jackie O.*, and *Elizabeth Taylor: The Last Star*, two nonfiction supersellers. In a speech to the American Society of Journalists and Authors in New York in May of 1982, Kelley advised fiction and nonfiction writers to avoid splashing mud on people's reputations, unless the writers are sure they can back up gossip with fact.

"I corroborate my information by interviewing people personally. I go only to people who know my subjects well, and like them a lot. I don't go to enemies. I don't want that kind of cruel testimony. I take a lot of notes and use tape recorders. Also, I read the entire public record, take notes on that, keep index cards, and start a filing system.

"I might start with the husbands; since Elizabeth Taylor had six of them, that was a big job. I went to MGM, her studio for twenty years, and they opened the files to me. I got names there [of people to interview], legal records and even dental records, [names of] producers, directors, co-stars, neighbors, hairdressers.

"Many people wouldn't talk to me, but a lot did cooperate. I did tell one man, 'Just tell me why you love Liz. I'm going to write the book anyway, so it will be better if you tell me that.' He did give me one super quote, even though he had started by telling me he wouldn't talk. The entire project—400 interviews and the writing—took three years.

"On corroboration: if you can't get the full scoop on an incident you hear about, you need some public record to back you up. I found out, for example, that Elizabeth Taylor and two male stars got drunk in the Plaza Hotel and destroyed the room because the Plaza wouldn't let Liz get away without paying her bill. They each denied it. But it had been reported to the police, so I got the information from the precinct records."

Letters are private, notes Dave Curran of Wisconsin. Be wary of reproducing letters sent to you by friends; they may not appreciate sharing their thoughts with the public. In a letter of his own to all writers in a national magazine, Curran reminded writers that copyright laws forbid them to reproduce letters someone sent to them unless that person grants specific permission.

Curran said that when you send a letter to someone—just as when you sell a painting—the recipient owns the physical letter or painting. But he does not own the right to reproduce that letter or painting unless the writer or painter who created the work gives him that right. Curran says, "Don't assume that if you own a letter someone has written, you can print whatever it says."

Never underestimate the wrath of "friends" who may feel they are unfairly depicted in your novels, warns Lou Isaf. And watch out for the greed of strangers who sniff out a potential legal weakness in your fiction and leap on it as a chance to make some money in court.

"A lot of writers want to base their characters on real people. They ask me, 'Can I do it?' No. Writers have often gotten away with some crazy depictions, but that doesn't mean they're not flirting with disaster. Stay on the safe side and keep away from using real people in your fiction.

"Even if you get permission from someone to use him or her in a novel, you're not protected. In fiction the writer never really knows what he'll end up saying. So the person who consents to let himself be used as a character isn't sure what he's consenting to. You are fairly safe if you use public figures, but sometimes that area gets shady; your defense is determined by the extent to which that person is deemed a public figure. Someone out of the public view has the right to remain that way. If you tamper with a person's privacy, you're opening yourself to a lawsuit.

"If you simply must base your character on a real person, disguise that character so the person can't recognize himself. If all you're going to use is the name, and nothing else is similar, you're probably safe. If the name is very unusual—like Isaf— you'd better get permission.

"Plagiarism is another area that worries writers. It's fuzzy, and sometimes only a jury can decide whether or not you purposely stole someone else's work. If you take another writer's unique phrase, or his creative way of saying something, you're in trouble. If you use 'once upon a time' from someone else, that's hardly unique, so you're not plagiarizing.

"Don't rely on the old saw that you're safe if you take fifty words or less. Both quantity *and* quality of the 'theft' are important. You may take five words of mine, but if they're five words that are very important to me and I can prove you diluted the value of my work by taking them, you're in trouble."

Publishers won't protect you, laments Gwen Davis. In 1980, Davis was sued, along with her publisher, Doubleday, by a California psychologist who claimed he was libeled in Davis's novel, *Touching*. The psychologist won and was awarded $75,000 by the courts. Then Doubleday turned around and sued the author for $1,000,000 to recoup its costs. The disagreement was settled out of court, but it left Davis and the community of writers badly shaken, she told *Publishers Weekly*.

"I know a lot of agents are turning down books because they are afraid, and publishers are turning down first novels because almost all first novels draw on experience [Davis's novel drew on her experience with the psychologist]. The only support that I really had was from the community of writers, who were wonderful. It took so much out of my life . . . [but] I have a new novel in the works, and I'm pleased to report I've found a heroic publisher: Arbor House."

What can you copyright? Kirk Polking, who has been an editor, writing teacher, and expert on copyright law for many years, says that some copyright protection is automatic.

"When you create writing, it is considered copyrighted by law, automatically and at once, at the moment of creation. The law says if you created it and can prove it's yours, you're protected.

"It's impossible to copyright a plot, ideas, facts, or news. You can only protect the *presentation* of that idea. The idea itself is common property.

"Protect your presentation by carbon copies, tape recordings, and research that shows you created the work. Put dates on everything. The copyright notice is ©, the year, and your name on the first page of the manuscript. For formal registration, write to the Copyright Office, Library of Congress, Washington DC 20559 (for form TX). It is formal proof of your ownership of the literary material you've created."

Avoid problems by working with an agent, advises Stuart Woods. Shopping for an agent in New York City, he landed Morton Jankelow, a man who, he feels, is one of the best in the field. Among other services, Jankelow negotiated a $50,000, three-part television series for *Chiefs*.

"I just didn't look in the phone book for an agent. I realized the agent would be the man or woman who could help me a lot—or not help—and I went about my search in a businesslike way.

"I asked my publisher to recommend three of the best agents in New York City. Then I went there to meet them personally. One didn't read my novel before he met me, so I discounted him at once. One I didn't feel comfortable with; it was a personality thing. I got along really fine with the other man and his reputation was the best, so he became my agent.

"This man was not Jankelow. He came later. I used my first agent for some time, but when I felt the need to sever our professional relationship, it was done with no hard feelings. Sometimes you have to move on. He had done some work on *Chiefs* so he was entitled to compensation, and we wound up agreeing on five percent. Jankelow took over from there. I pay fifteen percent for him, but he's also an attorney, so I'm paying for his legal fees as well as for his extraordinary skill in getting me the best possible deal.

"To get an agent like Jankelow, you need to have established a reputation of your own, or have something awfully good in manuscript form to show. Let more than one agent read your work. Then if several of them like what you do, you have a choice.

"Make that choice on a businesslike basis. Yes, I felt I had to get along with my agent, so personality was a factor. But most of all I was looking for an aggressive person who was willing to take risks on my behalf and who would be my advocate: a person willing to fight for me, even at the expense of his own relationship with a publisher."

Agents can't be timid, laughs Bill Diehl. He tells the

story of his first and wildly successful novel, *Sharky's Machine*, as an example of a "gutsy chance" his agent had to take on his behalf with skeptical publishers.

"I met my first agent, Freya Manston, on a New York City street corner. We were introduced rather casually by a friend I was visiting at the time. She told me to send her something, and I sent her an article I'd written for a local magazine. She called and said it was good; why didn't I try fiction?

"I didn't have the time to do that. But it just so happened that I was later called to jury duty, and I had a lot of time to sit around and be bored, waiting to be picked. So I borrowed a pen and a legal pad from a law clerk and started writing, and it turned out to be chapter six of *Sharky*.

"It had been two years since I met Freya. But I called her anyway, and she remembered me. I told her I had a chapter of something, and explained my idea for a plot, and she urged me to do an outline and 120 pages. The outline was only six pages long. I couldn't write more, because I had no idea how the story would go on. So at the end of the outline I wrote, 'That's all I'll tell you for now.'

"That was terribly flip. Some publishers, seeing that from a totally unknown writer, would throw an agent back into the streets. But Freya pulled it off. She got them to think this was a really mysterious writer with a hot plot, and she sold it for $156,000."

Agents take risks. They're paid to do that for writers, and they also do it because the agent is the writer's best friend, remarks Anne Rivers Siddons.

"Too often, writers take a lot of time trying to form close personal relationships with editors. I think their energy should be spent in trying to make friends with an agent, instead.

"I don't think it's as necessary to have a deep personal relationship with an editor as it is to have one with an agent. You do change editors and publishing houses. If possible, however, you should stay with one good agent forever.

"The agent's career rises and falls with yours. He or she only makes money if you make money. The agent puts his neck out for you; publishers won't always do that. If you have only one literary friend, let it be your agent."

Payment for agents should be only 10 percent of what you earn, recommends the Author's Guild. The Guild surveyed top agents in 1981 and found that most charged a fee of 10 percent for fiction and nonfiction writers who showed promise. A few charged higher rates for all the shopping around entailed in a first novel, but only a few raised fees to 15 percent for all clients. The Guild says that's too much.

"The saving effect by not using an agent may more than compensate for any income lost by not getting the last possible royalty percentage point that an agent may obtain. To many authors, an agent at 15 percent may simply not be worth it."

Agents are worth 15 percent, argues agent Arnold Goodman of New York. He notes that agents read your work, find a suitable publisher for it, negotiate a contract, help with publicity, and are essential to a writer's career. For all this work, he says, 15 percent of the author's "take" is a reasonable fee, because agents work very hard and don't see much return for their efforts. The work goes on long after the book is sold, says Goodman. Good agents wll enhance a writer's career by dealing with the author-editor relationship, promotion and publicity, subsidiary rights, and even help the author plan other books to enhance his career.

"It's not a one-shot deal. It's a relationship. We spend a lot of time with our clients, and that puts a limit on how many clients we can take. We're running a boutique, not a department store."

Writers can be easily cheated without an agent, warns Irving Kaler, an attorney and author's advocate who serves as advisor, agent, buddy and joke-teller to top Southeastern writers. Kaler, whose clients call him "Uncle Irving," says the agent's biggest job is to negotiate a tight contract for the author.

"A good writer should expect that his book will make a movie, and when you talk about that you're talking big money. You can get badly stung if you try to do a contract alone, or if your agent or lawyer doesn't know his way around. Check for these things in a contract: are you keeping the movie and TV rights? Don't sign a form contract that gives these rights to the publisher. Are you getting a hefty part of the foreign rights? Sometimes publishers try to escalate their profits on these sales. What do the movie rights include: are you getting a share of anything sold to cable or on discs? If you're not sure, ask. If your agent is not sure, why is he your agent?"

Check up on your agent, advises R.V. Cassill. Ask other authors about the agent's reputation. Ask the agent for a list of authors he represents, and for permission to query the authors about him. Then, ask publishers with whom the agent deals if the agent is expert and reputable. The most important check is if the agent performs well in negotiating your contract. Cassill says authors should check these points in their contracts:

"Be sure the publisher can't reclaim the advance if he decides not to publish your book after you deliver the manuscript, as long as you've turned in a good piece of work on time.

"Does the publisher have any claims on your next book? If he does, will you be well paid for giving him the chance to work with you again?

"In case of a libel charge, will the publisher defend you, stand with you, and share the responsibility?

"What are the resale, paperback, and book club rights?

"Are you getting at least fifty percent of foreign resale rights?

"What are the serial rights? First serial rights for a portion of the book means a magazine or newspaper can print the work before the book comes out. Second serial means the reprint happens after the book comes out. Make sure you get paid extra for these.

"Do you ask the publisher to commit to spending a certain amount for publicity, and is it specified in the contract?

"If you have to travel to do research for the book, will the publisher pay your expenses?

"An agent should go over all these points with you. If he doesn't, something is wrong. Ask, and if the agent appears defensive or confused, find another agent. Don't compromise on your contract."

You can have a contract with an agent, Cassill adds. "Most agents work without contracts, and this is the best way for you because if things go wrong you can slip easily out of the relationship. If you do sign a contract with an agent, check on these points: 1) Is it only for fiction? Only for books, or for poems, articles, and the like? 2) Is it for one book, two books, or forever? 3) Can you leave if the agent doesn't produce quickly?"

Return the advance? It sounds horrible, but agent Caroline Harkleroad says publishers are sometimes entitled to get their money back. Harkleroad spent nine years as a New York publicist before becoming an agent.

"There are three major points that agents fight about in contracts, and there's a lot of disagreement and confusion among the agents themselves about these points.

"First is, if the publisher rejects the manuscript after it's written, should the author have to give back the advance money? Most agents say no. I say, very possibly yes.

"If an editor has problems so severe with a manuscript that it can't be published, the writer should return the money. I have great faith in editors; they don't reject your work on a whim. If the manuscript under contract is rejected, in my experience it has generally been the fault of the writer, and the money should be returned.

"There are certain circumstances where the writer obviously tried his best to do a good job, but simply couldn't turn out a book. In that case the writer should keep the money; it was a good faith try. But in my experience, too many authors land a contract on an outline, then figure they've got it made. They fool around, delay like crazy, and do a lousy job because they think they can turn in just anything and keep at least 40 percent on the advance. They do themselves and the writing profession a great injustice. I know many other agents will disagree with me, but in the long run I think the writers of the world are better protected if they don't have a 'no return' clause in their contracts.

"The next important clause in the contract says that the work can be rejected after it's done if it's not 'satisfactory to the publisher.' Some agents want to substitute, 'the manuscript shall be professionally competent and fit for publication.' I don't think the change in terminology helps, so I don't insist on such changes. Both terms are subject to interpretation, and I think it's important for agents to concentrate instead on other clauses, rather than wasting time on this one.

"The clause upon which I absolutely insist is that the contract must clearly state [that] if the manuscript is rejected, you get a written statement within sixty days of the rejection telling you exactly *why* you got turned down, and giving you another sixty days to make changes so you get another chance."

You can go it alone, writers Stephen Goldin and Kathleen Sky told authors in an article they did for a national magazine. It does take time and knowledge, but writers can do without an agent. The pair said writers can learn to market their own work, negotiate with editors, and build their own careers. In the movie and TV world, however, agents are essential.

"In movies and TV you *must* have an agent; producers refuse to even look at unagented material. But in the publishing world there are only a few things agents can do that are difficult or impossible for you to do on your own, like maintain overseas connections to sell foreign rights, or conduct an auction of your work."

Foreign rights are yours, overseas agent Norman Bloom reminds writers. Bloom, of Solo News Network of London, helps American writers who want to make a killing on overseas sales.

"The author should get full percentage of foreign rights, less whatever the agent charges. I take 20 percent on these. The publisher might overlook foreign sales, and it's not likely he'll be able to sell the rights himself. The way to be sure you're getting the best deal in foreign rights is to hire an aggressive agent who can show you he has a presence in the overseas market. Count his overseas sales as part of an agent's credentials when you make the choice of who will represent your work."

12 | The Writing Life

THE FICTION WRITER'S LIFE swells and plunges like a roller coaster. You're high when writing is easy and manucripts sell; you fall when words won't come and publishers turn away.

It takes a tough, flexible, determined, and highly disciplined personality to make it as a professional writer. The writing life is unstable; you must provide emotional and financial anchors of your own. There is little guarantee of a steady paycheck, and you have to plan ahead for your own insurance, vacation money, retirement funds, and other benefits. To keep afloat, you must continually produce chunks of excitement—in the form of words on paper—for consumption by strangers.

WHY DO PEOPLE WRITE?

If it's so tough, why do people want to write? Many professionals admit they're in it for the money. The Author's Guild recently published a survey by three Columbia University professors showing that writers of fiction earned an average of $50,000 per year. The royalties and movie rights from just one good book might set you up for life.

But only about 5 percent of all writers make a good living on full-time fiction. The same survey revealed that the median income for the 2,239 authors involved was $4,775 per year. These writers make a living with other jobs—mostly teaching—and write after work or on weekends. Their incomes from writing are not heavily counted on to fatten the family coffers.

MONEY ISN'T EVERYTHING

Obviously, then, money isn't the prime reason most people write. Non-professionals may turn to their typewriters at the end of the day to let out frustrations over boring jobs or bad marriages. Some people just enjoy the act of writing fine prose and reading it to themselves. The thrill for these writers comes from *doing*, not publishing. They are spared the knuckle-whitening terror that paralyzes the professional when a publisher says no, and months or years of unpaid work seems in danger of sliding away.

Some people say they put words on paper to assert themselves. LeAnn Schreiber of *The New York Times* thinks women, especially, do this, even though it's harder for them to display their feelings in black and white.

"Before the twentieth century, even the act of picking up the pen, of claiming Adam's right to name and define things, implied a degree of self-assertion that made a woman a suspect member of her sex, an overreacher like Eve," says Schreiber.

Other writers tell me they are motivated by hard-to-explain artistic impulses, the need to express pent-up feelings, a simple love of language, or a desire to contribute something to humanity. Robert Coram says he writes because he wants to be published, but also because "I'm idealistic, and some day

I'll write something that will change a person's life. That sure and certain belief is what spurs me on."

DISCIPLINE DOES IT

Coram and other writers who want to publish their work rely on an important personality trait to channel their motives so writing is produced. That trait is *discipline*. It takes discipline to think up ideas, get them organized and down on paper, and push until they're published. My definition of a professional writer is one who relies on the money he makes by publishing his work, and all professionals are disciplined. A lot of writers won't talk about that part of their lives, because discipline isn't glamorous. But if a book is produced, you know discipline did it.

The ability to force yourself to perform the creative act is a must for professionals. And professionals learn to edit so that the end product doesn't look forced, because they're forging careers with every paragraph. A career, by definition, is a money-making enterprise. If you want to be a writing professional, steady production for the marketplace has to happen whether or not you're in the mood. Writing can be your joy . . . but it must also be your business.

BE YOUR OWN BOSS

If you decide to define writing in those terms, you can approach a story, novel, poem, or article very much as if it is part of a nine-to-five job. I do. I organize my day in chunks of time, allowing a set amount of hours to complete a specific writing job. That way I force myself to keep deadlines, and make sure my work is constantly circulating to magazines and publishing houses. This takes tremendous self-discipline, because nobody is in the office urging me on or complaining if I don't perform. I must be my own stern boss.

My day begins at seven a.m., when I rise to fix breakfast for my husband and two children. When the family leaves at eight I clean the house, then munch on bran muffins while I'm clipping the newspaper for story ideas. By nine I'm in my blue-carpeted office upstairs, writing. I stop for about twenty minutes of jogging, then lunch, and I'm back at my writing until the children come home from school at four p.m. The last hour of my working day is reserved for telephoning editors and answering mail.

This routine is broken by forays to the library or visits to interview someone for an article or story. But self-imposed interruptions come infrequently, because most of the time I struggle to make the length and form of my days much the same as those of a businessperson. I know other writers who sleep, play tennis, or shop during the day, and write for about six hours at night. Each person sets up his own routine. The critical thing is to *have* a routine. A professional must summon up the self-discipline to create and follow daily writing patterns.

Discipline is the primary demand of the writing life. Hayes B. Jacobs, who advises many new writers, says "Forget the chatter about 'mood' and 'inspiration.' Set up some daily routine, and stick to it . . . Without discipline on the part of the writer, nothing gets written."

* * *

Talent fades without discipline, remarks Paul Hemphill. His first novel, *Long Gone*, came after twenty years of writing magazine articles and nonfiction books.

"Talent is part God-given gift and part education. But it goes nowhere without discipline. Discipline makes you sit down in front of the damned typewriter and produce something to sell. It makes you quit yakking on the phone with friends, and get to work.

"If you can't get enough peace and quiet at home, find an

office. I once rented ground-floor space in an old hotel. My typewriter and reference books were there, and I went to it every day like I was going to a job. It was quiet, and there was a place across the street when I got hungry. I wrote off the rent for income taxes.

"Eventually I moved back home, but having an office reinforced my sense of discipline. I set up a home office just like it, and I'm forced to write when I get in there because there's nothing else for me to do in that room.

"The other thing that forces me to write is a need to make money. I support a lot of kids. My first novel didn't make that much of an advance, but it's been bought as a movie and I'll get $50,000 the first day the filming starts.

"Writing is one funny way to make a living. It's feast and famine, up and down, and if you can't stand that kind of insecurity you'd better do something else. I know writers who make $5,000 a year and writers who make $50,000. You can't count on any solid figure. It fluctuates wildly. The best you can count on is a rough approximation of minimum wages at first.

"You'll get about $250 per short story. Try to figure out how much you need to write and sell per year to stay alive. Hopefully you'll go on from there to several thousand per story, and big bucks for books.

"It can happen if you discipline yourself to write on a routine basis, and especially to overcome the natural fears all writers have."

Fear haunts even the best-known writers,

admits Broadway playwright Neil Simon. In 1981 he told *The New York Times* that writing is fun, but it still puts him in a cold sweat.

"When I go to work in the morning I read the newspaper first. I don't have the slightest idea of what I'm going to do. I'm in this meditative mood. It's like being on a high board, looking down to a cold, chilly pool. Then I give myself a little push. The water isn't as cold as I thought. I don't think anyone gets writer's block. I think fear takes over."

You can conquer writer's fear, maintains Stuart Woods.
It sometimes takes years, but fear of failure can be overcome by a writer with discipline and courage.

"First, I was afraid of being alone. I had come from a public relations job in a busy office, and I was scared of the solitude. But I just forced myself to organize my days, and it wasn't long before I learned to enjoy the isolation.

"Next I had to overcome the writer's biggest fear: failure. I had told my friends I was writing a novel, and I wondered, 'What if I can't do it?' I started *Chiefs* in 1973, and put it aside for several years because I was afraid of failure. I did two nonfiction books instead: one about sailing, and one on travel. When I got to feeling sure of myself I went back to the novel, and I was able to finish. I learned that a writer can—*must*—keep cool and conquer fear in order to write."

A cool head is necessary to view your own work,
according to Truman Capote. He calls writing "nerve-shattering," a "continuous, constant gamble." Long ago he told an interviewer that he strips himself of emotion when he writes in order to achieve control and look at his own product with detachment.

"Dickens, as he wrote, choked wth laughter over his own humor and dripped tears all over the page when one of his characters died. My own theory is that the writer should have considered his wit and dried his tears long, long before setting out to evoke smilar reactions in a reader. In other words, I believe the greatest intensity in art in all its shapes is achieved with a deliberate, hard, and cool head."

A writer's head is shaped in childhood, contends Terry Kay. He says his novels of the South spring from tales he heard as a child, then re-formed as an adult.

"A good adult writer was probably a good child listener. Kids who pay attention to stories they hear, who can sit quietly and absorb plot and fantasy, might have the best chance to be writers. I didn't tell good stories on the front porch back home. I *listened*. First you are a story-listener. Then you are a storyteller. When I was a kid, the best stories were told by the old folks in their rocking chairs on the front porch after supper. My big break in writing was probably that we had a very large front porch."

After childhood come the lean years, says Paul Boles. There is usually no escape from those first, hungry years of writing, when you toil alone without knowing if your work will ever be published, or your efforts paid.

"I wrote my first novel, *The Streak*, in 1953. It was done without an outline and without any promises from anyone about whether or not it would ever see the light of day. I'd carried the idea around in my head for years, so when I sat down in front of the fireplace to write it, it just felt right, and I was able to finish in a few weeks.

"The first publisher I sent it to turned it down, saying I didn't know anything about my subject. That was a hungry time. But eventually my book sold and it was optioned for a movie. I made $50,000 on it over the next three or four years. Then for the next ten years I wrote almost nothing except short stories. My price for the stories in the mid-50s was $2,500, and it still is.

"If I got nothing but the original price for these stories I'd need to write and sell about one story every three weeks in order to live the way I want to live. But a story, or a book, doesn't end its life with first publication if it's good. It's picked up in

Italian, French, Swedish. There are foreign rights and subsidiary rights. And it gets put in anthologies and textbooks; money comes in from these. I get a check every now and then for such spin-offs. It's not much—say $400 or so—but it adds up. My agent takes care of the more complicated stuff for me, but I lived through the hungry years and I did my first four novels with no agent at all.

"My advice to a beginning writer of fiction is to try and sell some short stories without an agent to a few good college or little literary magazines. They won't pay much, but that's not the purpose. If they publish your work, it will be seen by big-time New York editors, who constantly look for new writers this way. If they like your stories and ask you to send them something, they're in a position to pay quite a bit.

"As a writer you'll always have a fluctuating salary, and you have to be able to handle that by salting it away, when it comes in, for the lean times. A lot of writers somehow instinctively marry people who do this for them.

"It's not a richly endowed life, but it can surprise you and be quite comfortable. The important thing is to stop being self-conscious, screw up your confidence, and *write*."

Self-consciousness sometimes cripples female writers, says Erica Jong. She told interviewer John L. Kern that it's hard to live through "all the hate and personal character assassinations" that pass for book reviews by people who are threatened by the writing of assertive women. But unless you can tolerate such attacks, you may never say what's really on your mind.

"I think that I receive a lot of hostile notices because I have been held responsible for the emergence of women and female sexuality. Of course, it's not true. I only wish I were responsible; it would be a great honor. In any case, my work has been identified with women demanding rights in the bedroom, and

I think that many men and women had a lot of mixed feelings about that and it led them to attack my work.

"Our society is still very uncomfortable with the idea of successful women. Underneath all of the lip service that this country gives to the women's movement, I belive that it is still very sexist. So, if a woman is conspicuous and writes about sex and makes a lot of money, both men and women tend to be very hostile toward her."

Express feelings honestly, even if it hurts, says poet and novelist Rosemary Daniell. Her book, *A Sexual Tour of the Deep South*, enraged some editors and readers because it hit a fever-pitch of emotion. But the feelings couldn't be suppressed, asserts Daniell. If they were, her writing would turn out to be bland and dishonest.

"Sex, lust, hate, violent anger: they're all real feelings. If you try to hide them you'll never reach your potential as a writer. If you're the kind of person who just can't let those feelings out, you shouldn't *be* a writer.

"That doesn't mean you have to be comfortable while you're expressing those feelings. Writing isn't a comfortable job. I certainly didn't feel at ease about opening up my innermost feelings for everyone to read in my poems, and later in novels. I even had nightmares about 'telling.' In the South, especially, telling on your family and neighbors is taboo, and I certainly told. On the night I signed the contract for one of my books, I dreamed I'd been shot and killed. It was punishment for getting ready to let all those pent-up feelings come out in my writing.

"Women, especially Southern women like me (but I think all women in general), have been taught not to show feelings. We're supposed to keep smiling, and look pretty, and pretend everything is just fine. It's un-ladylike to write dirty words, or put down how you'd like to cut someone to bits.

"But if you want to be a writer of any consequence you must cast aside that early training in deception and let your feelings come out, no matter how vile and nasty and sweaty and sexy they may be. You'll learn not to be ashamed. And you'll find, as I did, that people won't condemn you for writing half as much as you think they will. If they do, it's their problem.

"A good writer can't be afraid of feelings. Make the decision to tell it all. Then, follow through."

Follow-through is critical, says editor and writer J. Michael Robertson. He says publishers are antagonized by writers who don't deliver what they promise. That's one reason why publishers prefer to see a writer's work rather than hear his discussions of that work; if it's already on paper, the publisher can be certain the material exists. Robertson judged both fiction and nonfiction when he worked for a city magazine, and emphasizes that writers must have a stick-to-it personality.

"It *is* lonely and scary to work all day in a room by yourself, but if you do get started you must continue. A professional writer doesn't stay discouraged, doesn't stay down for long. Definite personality traits do stand out in the successful writer. You must be:

"*Tenacious*. You have to stick to the material until you get a manuscript or story out of it. Then you have to be stubborn enough not to fade if it gets rejected by one publisher, or by several of them. Quickly send it to someone else.

"*Enthusiastic,* even childlike in your love of words. You have to be eager to do your writing. That makes it easier to stick to a writing schedule, too. And can you imagine devoting your life to writing if you don't *love* what you're doing?

"*Observant*, as if you're seeing everything for the first time. That will keep your writing fresh, your descriptions vivid. Editors like freshness. They don't want tired words or pre-digested thoughts.

"*Flexible.* Not everything you write will be ideal. Sometimes you won't like something you write, but the editor likes it—so it stays. Or the editor may ask you to take something out you do like—and it comes out. You have to be flexible so you can accept an editor's suggestions. I don't mean be willing to follow slavishly, but be willing to learn to change.

"*Patient.* You need patience to research, then actually sit down long enough to organize the material and get it on paper. Remember that writing is a lot of nitty-gritty work. It's a rare person who gets it right the first time. Most stuff needs to be rewritten, so you need the patience to go over it once, twice, three times—even more. Then after all that you'll have to do some editing to correct spelling and grammar and sharpen sentences. Don't leave it to the editor; he won't enjoy cleaning up your mess.

"*Talented.* Of course you need talent and orginality. I think at least part of that is inborn; you either have it or you don't. But if you do have it you must be mature enough to use it properly, to know the difference between being original and being silly.

"Once I got a query letter from a writer asking me if I'd like to look at his story. His letter was handwritten—really a mess. It was a jumble of cross-outs and ink stains and crumpled paper. And at the end, this guy printed, 'When I turn in my story, it will look just the opposite of the way this letter looks.'

"I didn't ask to see the story. I didn't trust the writer. He was too cute. He was original, but he didn't know where the limits were. It's important to be talented, but you also need strong traits of maturity and discipline. Don't fall into the trap of being so desperate for attention that you resort to tricks like the one I just described.

"Look again at this list of personality traits. They are shared by every successful writer I know. If you have them, go for the writing life. You can do it."

Epilogue

THE WORK OF WRITING doesn't end with your last chapter. There will be galleys to read, corrections to make, last-minute changes that force themselves into your book. You can't even rest when you hold the finished product, neatly bound and jacketed, in your hands. Many writers say *that's* when the real work begins.

Writers must promote their own books, and the time and energy required is considerable. Unless your publisher takes over with a huge ad budget and a fighting force of in-house publicists equivalent to a small army, you'll have to wrestle as much free publicity as you can out of the media. Even huge promotional pushes from the publisher—with lots of money to back them up—require authors to travel, talk to garden clubs, appear on radio and television, show up at schools, and do everything they can to fuel interest in the book.

HAVING A GRAND TIME

It's easy to get overwhelmed, however. New writers have a grand time at first, dashing from TV studios to book-signing parties. But the grueling routine quickly wears thin. Paul Hemphill says, "My first time on a TV show, I got there two hours early. My second time, I was fifteen minutes early. Third time, I came right as they were going on the air. And my fourth time I overslept and almost missed the damned thing. It got boring."

Boredom might be the least of your problems. The writing community is always buzzing with horror stories about books that are published at the wrong season and never sell; books ignored by store owners and buried on dusty shelves; books reviled by reviewers; or books that are simply allowed to die by publishers who don't print enough copies, won't advertise, and never reprint them.

WHAT CAN YOU DO?

What can the writer do? Plenty. This epilogue will give you a few basic tips on getting to know the ins and outs of book publicizing. Use them to be sure that after you're published, you'll go on to do it again and again—successfully!

Hire a publicist and you'll have your own public relations specialist at your side. If possible, your agent should try to get publicity clauses in your contract. These clauses at the very least will assure you of some advertising for your book. Even the best book won't sell if it doesn't have the proper media exposure, so authors should try to find publishers who will guarantee a reasonable publicity budget in the contract.

Even better, the publisher might be persuaded to hire an independent publicist to work with you in promoting your book. You may have to pay part of the publicist's fee, but often the publisher picks up the entire tab. Even big publishing houses don't have the time, staff, or knowledge to publicize a book properly; their energy often goes into making a big deal out of the superstars.

That's why freelance publicity people are brought in to work closely with authors of promising books; part of their job is to tailor publicity to meet individual needs.

Writer Thomas Weyr has a good article on publicists, "Promoting from Without," in the January 1, 1982, issue of *Publishers Weekly*.

Epilogue

Make friends with book buyers. They are the people who can help make you successful by ordering your book in large quantities and displaying it in their stores. Buyer Faith Brunson, who has been a top buyer for Rich's, Inc., in Atlanta, for twenty-three years, is widely regarded as an expert in literature, and in what sells and doesn't sell.

"Don't overlook the book buyer and the book salesperson as a valuable writer's friend," she says. "The salesperson can 'make' your book by repeatedly recommending it to customers, or break it by not reading it and just letting it sit on the shelf.

"Of course, the book buyer—people like me—decides whether or not your book ever gets to the shelf. I'd say if I buy 500 copies of your book, it's an exciting buy. A big buy is 1,000 copies. A very big buy is 2,500 copies. And a spectacular buy is 10,000 copies. That was my largest single order. It can make an author."

Haunt the bookstores. That's the advice of Oxford Books manager Frank J. McGuire. He says bookstores can make a new author by ordering many copies of his book, displaying it well, holding signing parties, and 'pumping' the book by word of mouth.

"Authors have been publicized more than ever in the last ten years, but when all is said and done you find that an enthusiastic bookseller, telling customers to buy and read a certain book, is an author's best friend. Your best promotional tool is a bookseller who will keep the book in stock and promote by word of mouth.

"It's not easy to keep a book in stock. Most people don't realize this, but the bookstore can return any book to its publisher if the book doesn't sell. We just ship it back to the manufacturer. We get full credit for it. That's why publishers are careful not to print more books than they think will sell—fast!

"We're careful about our version of overruns, too. We try not to buy too many books. That's because returning books is a hassle, and we have to pay the postage. So you, the author, may go into a bookstore and not find your book in stock because it's cheaper for the store to under-order rather than over-order.

"If neither the bookstore nor the publisher can sell your book, leftover copies go to a remainder house. This house buys a book for about twenty-five cents and sells it for perhaps a dollar. A remainder house sells publisher's mistakes.

"The author can take some steps to see that doesn't happen to his book. First of all, make friends with your local bookstores and urge them to buy and stock your book. Then you have to be ready to tour, perhaps to bookstores in other cities, and be comfortable with strangers you'll meet that way. Try and force your publisher to pay for a tour, but if he won't, do it yourself if you possibly can.

"Selling books means going from city to city to pump them. Do book signings in bookstores on Saturdays, when people are out browsing. Haunt the bookstores. It pays off."

Keep your work alive by helping editors and publishers get book reviews. A few of the better-known magazines receptive to reviewing new fiction are: *Esquire* (reviewer James Wolcott); *Harper's* (Michael Kinsley); *Mother Jones* (Katha Pollitt and Elinor Langer); *The Nation* (Elizabeth Pocoda); *National Review* (Chilton Williamson, Jr., Executive Editor); *The Atlantic* (James Atlas); *The New Republic* (Jack Beatty); *Newsweek* (Peter Prescott); *Saturday Review* (Robert Harris); and *Time* (Paul Grey).

Regional and special-interest books have other reviewing outlets, too. Keep track of specialty magazines that might be interested in reviewing your book, and write to ask if they'd like to see a copy. Your publisher should furnish a free copy of your book to any reviewer you suggest. Here are three examples of small publications which eagerly receive review copies of new specialized books. You can find out about other regional and specialty review outlets from your local library or book shop.

Epilogue

Mystery Forum, a nationally syndicated column, wants to see suspense and crime-related books. Send copies to Bob Myers, *Mystery Forum*, 16503 Third St. N., Independence MO 64056.

Arts Journal wants to see books by authors from North Carolina, South Carolina, Virginia, and Tennessee. Send copies to the magazine c/o William Ryan, Publisher, 324 Charlotte St., Asheville NC 28801.

County Lines magazine will review books by authors from the region of southeastern Pennsylvania or northern Delaware. Copies should go to C.S. Townsend, 22 E. Market St., W. Chester PA 19380.

Local and national groups for writers can teach you how to promote your book. Some of these groups are:

Arizona Author's Association (workshops on book promoting), 1832 E. Osborn Rd., Phoenix AZ 85016;

Washington Independent Writers (workshops on royalties and author-editor relations), telephone (202)347-4973;

Publishers Publicity Association (media appearances and how to book them; might refer authors) c/o Julia Knickerbocker, Simon & Schuster, 1230 Avenue of the Americas, New York NY 10020.

Agents and editors will share the names of other groups with you. Watch for local classes in book promotion sponsored by universities and libraries, and quiz your librarian for more information.

Being published is fun if your book gets the attention you think it deserves. The following is a list of services that may help beat the drums for a good first or second book worthy of extra attention:

Sensible Solutions is a consulting firm that teaches authors how publishing works, and develops promotional strategies. If your book is in the "mid-list'" range (your publisher printed about ten thousand copies), the firm may be able to figure out ways to push it into the "blockbuster" range of a print run of twenty-five thousand or more. Publishers will often pay the firm's $3,000 fee. It is located at 14 E. Seventy-fifth St., Suite 5C, New York NY 10021; telephone (212)861-3693.

The Writer's Service is a similar consulting firm run by a former editor, Shelly Lowenkopf. You can reach him at Box 536, Summerland CA 93067; telephone (805)969-6092.

The Bookers works with literary agents to arrange interviews for authors, does press releases, and generally pushes good books. Authors pay a small surcharge for this extra attention. Ask your agent for details.

The University of California, Berkeley Extension, offers courses in book promotion for authors and also offers publishing workshops. Write UC Extension, 2223 Fulton St., Berkeley CA 94720; telephone (415)642-4111. Many other universities offer similar courses; you should check your local colleges and universities.

The American Writer's Congress was recently formed to help writers keep the publishing industry responsive to their needs, such as the need for better after-publication assistance. Members include Gay Talese, Donald Barthelme, Kurt Vonnegut, Toni Morrison, and other well-known authors. The address is GPO Box 1215, New York NY 10116; telephone (212)420-0608.

Index

Ace Paperpacks, 143
Action, 103, 104
Adams, Harriet, 112
Advance, 169-171
After Eli, 45, 63, 74
Agents, 148, 164, 165-167, 168
Airport, 40
Aleichem, Sholom, 123
Alleys of Eden, The, 138
American Law Institute, The, 158
American Legal Publications, Inc., 158
American Short Story: An Untold Tale, The, 128
American Society of Journalists and Authors, 158, 160, 161
American Writers Congress, 136, 190
Anecdotes, 63
Apple-Wood Books, 140
Aptitude testing, 29
Arbor House, 138
Arizona Author's Association, 189
Armer, Alan, 111
Articles, 49-50
Arts Journal, 189
Ashmead, Larry, 55, 78, 105
Atlanta Constitution, 40, 107-108
Atlanta Journal, 107-108
ATLANTA magazine, 52
Atlantic Monthly, 101, 125, 188
Atlas, 38

Atlas, James, 188
Authenticity, 55
Author's Guild, 167, 173
Author's League, 157, 159
Autopsy, 65

Baker, John, 136
Banking on Death, 62
Barnes, Margaret Ann, 102, 153
Barthelme, Donald, 122, 125
Bartlett, John, 40
Barton, Clara, 58
Beattie, Ann, 125
Beatty, Jack, 188
Beginning Writer's Answer Book, The, 126
Berg, A. Scott, 136
Bible, 45
Big Stick Productions, 139
Biographies, 61
Bishop, Michael, 66
Block, Lawrence, 38, 47, 91-92, 98, 124
Blood Innocence, 27
Blood Tie, 80
Bloom, Norman, 171
Bodysculpture, 136
Boggess, Louise, 126
Boles, Paul Darcy, 19, 29, 101, 132, 156, 179
Bookers, The, 190

Books, 40-41
  buyers of, 187
  selling of, 187, 188
Bookstores, 187
Booze, 110
Borges, Jorge Luis, 122
Brady, John, 73
Brewer-Giorgio, Gail, 50
Brewer's Dictionary of Phrase and Fable, 40
Brown University, 31
Brun-Cottan, Francoise, 139
Brunson, Faith, 187
Business of writing, 17
Butler, Robert Olen, 138
Buyers of books, 187
"By-Line," 130

Calderella, Susan, 146
Caldwell, Erskine, 17
Capote, Truman, 28, 84, 127, 178
Cassill, R. V., 31, 51, 65, 98, 111, 119, 126, 129, 144, 168
Cat's Cradle, 113
Censorship, 156, 157
Centennial, 56
Chameleon, 42, 120
Chapin, Kim, 152
Characters, 69-81, 83-84, 87, 88, 89-90, 93-94, 123
  composite, 77
Chicago, 126
Chiefs, 30, 81, 106, 116, 165, 178
Children, My Children, 40
Cioffari, Phillip, 159
Cold Hands, 136
Collier, James Lincoln, 41
Collier's, 121
Columbia University, 75, 173
Committee to Restore Artistic Freedom to Authors, The (CRAFTA), 157-158
Composite characters, 77
Comprehensive Word Guide, The, 40
Computers, 33

Conflict, 88
Conroy, Pat, 37
Consent, 78
Consultants, 36
Contracts, 153, 168, 169
Cook, Tom, 27, 87, 103, 119
Copiers, 42
Copyright, 164
Coram, Robert, 49, 50, 174
Core, George, 123
Correction system, 34
County Lines, 189
Courses in journalism, 23
Covici, Pascal, 138
CRAFTA. *See* Committee to Restore Artistic Freedom to Authors
Craft of Interviewing, The, 73
Craft of writing, 17
Crawford, Tad, 37
Creation, 61
Criticism services, 26
Crossing in Berlin, 85
Cunningham, Chet, 146
Curran, Dave, 162
Current Biography, 58
Cutler, Bill, 75

Dance Card, The, 65
Daniell, Rosemary, 181
Darby's Gorilla, 44
Davis, Gwen, 163
Day of the Jackal, The, 52
Day No Pigs Would Die, A, 88
Dead Zone, The, 92
Deductions, 37
Defense, 160
Dial Press, 152
Dictionary of American Biography, 58
Dictionary of American Slang, 41
Diehl, Bill, 42, 70, 89, 103, 119, 127, 165
Discipline, 175
Dixie Council of Authors and Journalists, 24
Dog Soldiers, 93-94

Index

Doubleday, 163
Down These Mean Streets, 157
Drew, Nancy, 112
Dubus, Andre, 125, 134
Duncan, Lois, 48

Edgar Allan Poe Award, 27
Editors, 105, 129, 133, 135-153
Editor's Book Award, 137
Electric typewriter, 35
Elizabeth Taylor: The Last Star, 161
Elliott, Helen, 141
Emerson, Bill, 24-25, 133
Emotions, 80
Encyclopedia Britannica, 158
Endings, 100, 104-105
Endurance, 109
Esquire, 125, 133, 188
Executioner's Song, The, 56, 57
Exodus, 59
Expenses, 41-42
Experiences, 46-47, 91

Fact sheets, 56
Familiar Quotations, 40
Farrar, Straus & Giroux, 139, 148
Faulkner, William, 121
Fawn, 88
Feegel, John, 65
Feliciano, Jose, 58
Fiction Writer's Market, 126
Films, 42, 110
Fine, Don, 138
Fizgerald, F. Scott, 121
Flag for Sunrise, A, 94
Flame of New Orleans, 80
Flexner, 41
Foreshadowing, 92
Formula ideas, 45
Forsyth, Frederick, 52
Fox's Earth, 39, 93, 104, 117
Frank, Leo, 64, 77
Freeman, Cynthia, 138
Free press, 156
French Connection, The, 50

Fuller, Chet, 76

Georgia State University, 15
Gilmore, Gary, 56, 57
Giroux, Robert, 139, 148
God's Little Acre, 18
Golbitz, Pat, 106
Goldin, Stephen, 171
Goodman, Arnold, 167
Go Slowly, Come Back Quickly, 53
Gothics, 49, 60, 143
Grammar rules, 23
Graubart, Cliff, 149
Grey, Paul, 188
GR&F Royalty Auditing Firm, 158

Hailey, Arthur, 40, 56, 66
Hall, Donald, 139
Hall of Mirrors, A, 93
Handke, Peter, 122
Harkleroad, Caroline, 169
Harper & Row, 55, 78, 105
Harper's, 188
Harris, Jean, 107
Hawaii, 56
Heartbreak Hotel, 93
Hemingway, Ernest, 24, 34, 73, 129
Hemphill, Paul, 72, 176, 185
Hennissart, Martha, 62
Hero Ain't Nothing But a Sandwich, A, 157
Historical romance, 49
Hoban, Russell, 111
Horizon Press, 138
Hotel, 40, 56
Human Engineering Laboratory, Johnson O'Connor Research Foundation, 29

Ideas, 71, 87
  formula, 45
  story, 44
I Hear Them Calling My Name, 76

In Cold Blood, 28
Insurance, 159
Integrity, 142-143
International Paper Company, 113
International Women's Writing Guild, 158
Interviews, 62, 72-73
Irving, John, 85
Isaf, Louis, 78, 162

Jackie O., 161
Jacobs, Hayes B., 176
Jailbird, 113
Jankelow, Morton, 164
Johnson O'Connor Research Foundation, 29
Jong, Erica, 180
Journalism, 99
   courses in, 23
Joyce, James, 70, 113
Jurjevics, Juris, 152

Kaler, Irving, 168
Kansas City *Star*, 24
Kay, Terry, 45, 63, 70, 74, 114, 179
Keene, Carolyn, 112
Kelley, Kitty, 161
Kern, John L., 180
Kerr, Walter, 113
Keyes, Edward, 50
Kid with Heart, The, 101
King, Stephen, 92
Kinsley, Michael, 188
Kirk's Lane, 88
Knebel, Fletcher, 85
Knight, Damon, 79, 92, 116
Koontz, Dean R., 90, 101, 114

Ladies Home Journal, 133
Lange, Jack, 64, 77, 129
Langer, Elinor, 188
Lanier word processor, 36
Lassie Come Home, 30

Lathen, Emma, 62
Latsis, Mary Jane, 62
Lawliss, Chuck, 29
Laws on libel, 159
Lead, 99
LeCarre, John, 37
Legal defense, 160
Letters, 162
Lewis, Norman, 40
Libel Defense Resource Center, 158
Libel laws, 159
Library, 58-59
Library of Congress Copyright Office, 164
Life experiences, 46-47, 91
Literary agents, 148, 164, 165-167, 168
Literary Market Place, 25-26
Living Novel, The, 18
Lizotte, Ken, 160
Long Beach State College, 39
Long Gone, 72, 73, 176
Lords of Discipline, The, 37
Love stories, 49, 53

Magician, The, 94
Magic Mountain, 70
Mailer, Norman, 56
Major, Michael, 160
Malpractice, 66
Mann, Thomas, 70
Manston, Freya, 166
Markets, 47
Marquand, J. P., 121
McCall's, 133
McGuire, Frank J., 187
Mee, Charles L. Jr., 85
Melville, Herman, 31
Michener, James A., 56, 58
Middleton, Thomas H., 23
Mobil Travel Guides, 38
Mood, 101-102
Moore, Gene-Gabriel, 130, 150
Morrison, Henry, 137
Morrow, William, 106

Index

Mother Jones, 188
Motivation, 70-71
Movies, 42, 110
Murder in Coweta County, 102
Mystery Forum, 189
Mystery Writers of America, 27

Naked Ape, The, 157
Nation, The, 188
National Book Award, 80, 94
National Review, 188
Near, Jay, 156
Near v. Minnesota, 155-156
Nelson Algren Award, 126
New Republic, The, 188
Newspapers, 51
Newsweek, 188
New Yorker, 122, 125, 128
New York Times, 113, 128, 134, 174, 177
New York Times Book Review, 31, 56, 80
New York Times Manual of Style and Usage, 40, 143
New York University, 23
Niven, David, 53
No Enemy But Time, 66
Nonfiction, 49-50, 76-77
North Point Press, 140
Norton Anthology of Short Fiction, The, 31, 125
Norton Books, 151
Notes From Another World, 44
Novels, 47

Oates, Joyce Carol, 31, 122
O'Brien, Barbara, 147
Obscenity, 157
Observations, 29, 65
O'Connor, Frank, 123
O'Hara, John, 133
O. Henry Award, 125
Old New York Book Shop, 149
Olivetti, 41

Olmstead, Frederick Law, 61
Omni, 125
Ordinary People, 144
Organization, 93-94, 147
Orion, 50
Outlines, 85, 87, 90-91, 92, 93
Oxford Books, 187

Park Maker, 61
Peachtree Publishers, 140, 141, 151
Peck, Robert Newton, 88, 104, 115
PEN (The Author's League), 157
Penthouse, 159
Perkins, Maxwell, 150
Perry, Robin, 41
Personal observations, 29, 65
Phillips, Judson, 124
Photographs, 39
Pintauro, Joseph, 136
"Pitcher, The," 125
Plagiarism, 163
Planning, 83, 85-86
Playboy, 133
Plot, 88, 89-90, 91
Pocoda, Elizabeth, 188
Poe Edgar Allan, 121
Polking, Kirk, 164
Pollitt, Katha, 188
Pound, Ezra, 139
Practising Law Institute, 158
Preppies, 138
Prescott, Peter, 188
Princeton University Library, 160
Printers, 36
Promotional tools, 187
Proust, Marcel, 70
Publicists, 186
Public Nuisance Act of 1925, 156
Publishers, 90-91, 163-164
Publishers Publicity Association, 189
Publishers Weekly, 25, 29, 41, 50, 56, 164, 186
Purdue University, 31
Pushcart Press, 137, 140

Ragtime, 81
Reader's Digest-University of South Carolina writer's workshop, 25
Reading, 30, 31
Realism, 122
Reality, 40
Redbook, 125, 132
Remembrance of Things Past, 70
Rendering, 111
Research, 55-67
Reynolds, Burt, 42
Richard Rogers Bowker Memorial Lecture, 148
Rich's, Inc., 187
Riddley Walker, 111
Rip-Saw, 156
Robertson, J. Michael, 182
Rodale Books, 40
Romances, 49, 53
Romantic sagas, 80
Romeo and Juliet, 45
Ross, Michelle, 108
Royster, Vermont, 30
Rules of grammar, 23

Sagas, 80
Sales, 137
Saturday Evening Post, 121, 132, 133
Saturday Press, 156
Saturday Review, 188
Schreiber, LeAnn, 174
Science fiction, 66
Secretaries, 34
Secrets and Suprises, 125
Segal, Jonathan, 136
Self-education, 28-29
Selling of books, 188
Sensible solutions, 189
Settle, Mary Lee, 80
Seven Days in May, 85
Seven Hills of Paradise, 64
Seventeen, 132
Sewanee Review, 123
Sexual Tour of the Deep South, A, 181
Shakespeare, William, 113

Sharkey's Machine, 42, 89, 166
Short stories, 121-134
Shreve, Anita, 128
Shyness, 74
Sibley, Celestine, 40, 45, 46, 109
Siddons, Anne Rivers, 39, 72, 93, 104, 117, 148, 156, 166
Simon, Neil, 177
Simon & Schuster, 136
Simpson, Rosemarie, 63
Singer, Isaac Bashevis, 123
Sky, Kathleen, 171
Slaughterhouse Five, 113, 157
Slush pile, 128, 144
Smiley's People, 37
Smith-Corona, 33
Solo News Network, 171
Solzhenitsyn, Alexandr, 43
Sorrels, Roy, 39
Soul on Ice, 157
Sparrow Press, 31
Spikol, Art, 117
Statham, Frances, 49, 60, 79-80, 107, 118, 142
Stefanile, Felix, 31
Steinbeck, John, 138-139
Stein & Day publishing, 94
Stein, Sol, 94
Stevenson, Elizabeth, 61
Stone, Robert, 71, 93
Story ideas, 44
Stranger With My Face, 48
Streak, The, 179
St. Simons Island, 24
Style, 114, 116, 129
Susann, Jacqueline, 70
Suspense, 102-103
Sutherland, Mark, 36
Synonym Finder, The, 40
Synopsis, 144

Talent, 176-177
Tape recorders, 39, 63, 119
Tax deductions, 37
Taylor, Elizabeth, 162

Index

Taylor, Ron, 131
Teacher selection, 22-24
Team approach, 131
Teel Katy, 131
Teel, Len, 131
Telephones, 37
Telling Lies for Fun and Profit, 92
Testing of aptitude, 29
Themes, 46
Time, 188
Tobacco Road, 18
Tone, 101
Touching, 163
Tower Publications, 146
Treat, Lawrence, 91
Typewriters, 33, 34
    electric, 35
Typing services, 34

Ulysses, 70
Unemployment compensation, 160
University of California, 190
University of Chicago Press Manual of Style, The, 143
University of Michigan, 23-24
University of South Carolina, 25
Uris, Leon, 59

Valley of the Dolls, 70
Values, 52
Vanished, 85
Vidal, Gore, 61
Viking Press, 138, 144, 159
Vogue, 28

Vonnegut, Kurt, 113

Wall Street Journal, The, 38
Washington Independent Writers, 189
Watters, Pat, 62
Webster's New World Dictionary, 40
Wentworth, 41
West Coast Review of Books, 26
West, Jessamyn, 18
West Side Story, 45
Weyr, Thomas, 186
Wheels, 40
William Morris Agency, 143
Williams, Alan, 144
Williamson, Chilton Jr., 188
Winds of War, The, 81
Winn, William, 51
Wolcott, James, 188
Wolfe, Thomas, 85
Woods, Stuart, 30, 36, 45, 81, 87, 106, 116, 151, 164, 178
Woolf, Virginia, 31
Wood processors, 34, 35-36, 41
Workshops, 24-32
World According to Garp, The, 85
Wounded Birds, 45
Writer's Community, 28
Writer's Digest, 26, 31, 35, 117, 126, 146
Writer's Legal Guide, 37
Writer's Market, 143
Writer's Service, The, 190
Writing Fiction, 126
Writing the Novel from Plot to Print, 47, 98

Other Writer's Digest Books

General Writing Books
  Writer's Market, $18.95
  Beginning Writer's Answer Book, edited by Polking, et al $9.95
  How to Get Started in Writing, by Peggy Teeters $10.95
  Law and the Writer, edited by Polking and Meranus (paper) $7.95
  Make Every Word Count, by Gary Provost (paper) $6.95
  Teach Yourself to Write, by Evelyn Stenbock $12.95
  Treasury of Tips for Writers, edited by Marvin Weisbord (paper) $6.95

Magazine/News Writing
  Craft of Interviewing, by John Brady $9.95
  Magazine Writing: The Inside Angle, by Art Spikol $12.95
  Magazine Writing Today, by Jerome E. Kelley $10.95
  Newsthinking: The Secret of Great Newswriting, by Bob Baker $11.95
  Stalking the Feature Story, by William Ruehlmann $9.95
  Write On Target, by Connie Emerson $12.95
  Writing and Selling Non-Fiction, by Hayes B. Jacobs $12.95

Fiction Writing
  Fiction Writer's Help Book, by Maxine Rock $12.95
  Fiction Writer's Market, edited by Fredette and Brady $16.95
  Creating Short Fiction, by Damon Knight $11.95
  Handbook of Short Story Writing, edited by Dickson and Smythe (paper) $6.95
  How to Write Best-Selling Fiction, by Dean R. Koontz $13.95
  How to Write Short Stories that Sell, by Louise Boggess $9.95
  One Way to Write Your Novel, by Dick Perry (paper) $6.95
  Secrets of Successful Fiction, by Robert Newton Peck $8.95
  Writing the Novel: From Plot to Print, by Lawrence Block $10.95

Special Interest Writing Books
  Children's Picture Book: How to Write It, How to Sell It, by Ellen E.M. Roberts $17.95
  Complete Book of Scriptwriting, by J. Michael Straczynski $14.95
  How to Write and Sell Your Personal Experiences, by Lois Duncan $10.95
  How to Write & Sell (Your Sense of) Humor, by Gene Perret $12.95
  How to Write "How-To" Books and Articles, by Raymond Hull (paper) $8.95
  Mystery Writer's Handbook, edited by Lawrence Treat (paper) $8.95
  The Poet and the Poem, Revised edition by Judson Jerome $13.95
  Poet's Handbook, by Judson Jerome $11.95
  TV Scriptwriter's Handbook, by Alfred Brenner $12.95
  Travel Writer's Handbook, by Louise Purwin Zobel $13.95
  Writing and Selling Science Fiction, Compiled by The Science Fiction Writers of America (paper) $7.95
  Writing for Children & Teenagers, by Wyndham/Madison $10.95
  Writing to Inspire, by Gentz, Roddy, et al $14.95

The Writing Business
  Complete Handbook for Freelance Writers, by Kay Cassill $14.95
  How to Be a Successful Housewife/Writer, by Elaine Fantle Shimberg $10.95
  How You Can Make $20,000 a Year Writing, by Nancy Edmonds Hanson (paper) $6.95

Jobs for Writers, edited by Kirk Polking $11.95
Profitable Part-time/Full-time Freelancing, by Clair Rees $10.95
Writer's Survival Guide: How to Cope with Rejection, Success, and 99 Other Hang-Ups of the Writing Life, by Jean and Veryl Rosenbaum $12.95

To order directly from the publisher, include $1.50 postage and handling for 1 book and 50¢ for each additional book. Allow 30 days for delivery.

Writer's Digest Books, Department B
9933 Alliance Road, Cincinnati OH 45242
Prices subject to change without notice.